TABLE OF CONTENTS

INTRODUCTION

The "Shock and Awe" campaign that started the Second Iraq War on March 19, 2003 illustrated the latest attempt by leaders to replace a viable warfighting doctrine with the next "great idea." While the rapid collapse of Iraq seemed to validate the strategy of using a small invasion force, the lack of personnel to provide stability in postwar Iraq resulted in thousands of U.S. casualties, billions in spent treasure, and diminished international influence. On December 17, 2011, the last soldier left a still unsettled Iraq, challenging the soundness of basing this strategy on unproven concepts in lieu of established doctrine. Why did leaders advocate for untested concepts as the foundation for the war plan? This paper proposes the hypothesis "individual and group cognitive biases blind leaders into dogmatically advocating for inappropriate doctrine or unproven concepts in war planning and strategy development, resulting in a failure or delay in meeting national and military objectives."

Purpose

This thesis examines the role of individual and group cognitive biases on the decision making process used among senior political and military leaders, potentially contributing to decision error and misleading them into dogmatically advocating for inappropriate doctrine or unproven concepts in war planning and strategy development.

Methodology

This thesis evaluates four cases where leaders exhibited traits of individual and group cognitive biases in the process of planning for war. Chapter 1 provides the intellectual foundation for the analysis, offering definitions of doctrine, concept, and

1

dogma as well as a discussion of the relationship between doctrine and strategy. It then describes two individual cognitive biases most relevant to the military professional, describing anchoring and confirmation bias proposed by psychologists Daniel Kahneman and Amos Tversky in 1974. The chapter closes with a detailed discussion of antecedent conditions and symptoms of groupthink theory proposed by Irving Janis in 1982.[1]

Chapter 2 discusses two examples where leaders adhered to doctrine inappropriate for the conflict in which they fought. The first study describes the use of French "methodical battle" doctrine in World War II, when General Maurice G. Gamelin failed to recognized that the conditions for implementing French doctrine had changed, rendering it obsolete. The second study discusses U.S. attrition doctrine in the Vietnam War from 1965-1968, when General William C. Westmoreland adhered to "search and destroy" operations despite evidence of its ineffectiveness against a communist insurgency.

Chapter 3 presents two examples where leaders advocated for untested concepts and advanced technology masquerading as doctrine. The third study describes how Brigadier General Ira C. Eaker dogmatically followed the theory of unescorted "high altitude daylight precision bombing" in World War II, despite massive losses to B-17 formations in the skies over Germany in 1943.[2] The final study discusses the use of "rapid dominance" theory in the Second Iraq War, when Secretary of Defense Donald H.

---

[1] For more cognitive biases, see Daniel Kahneman and Amos Tversky, "Judgment under Uncertainty: Heuristics and Biases," *Science*, New Series, 185, no. 4157 (September 27, 1974), http://www.jstor.org/ stable/1738360 (accessed February 21, 2012); for more on groupthink, see Irving L. Janis, *Groupthink: Psychological Studies of Policy Decisions and Fiascos*, 2nd rev. ed. (Boston: Houghton Mifflin, 1983).

[2] This thesis focuses on "unescorted" high altitude daylight precision bombing (HADPB). For an indictment of HADPB as doctrine, see Peter R. Faber, "Interwar US Army Aviation and the Air Corps Tactical School: Incubators of American Airpower," *Paths of Heaven: The Evolution of Air Power Theory*, ed. Phillip S. Meilinger, (Maxwell Air Force Base, AL: Air University Press, 1987), 220-221.

Rumsfeld staunchly supported the employment of a smaller, highly technological force in place of a larger occupation force espoused by the Powell doctrine.

Chapter 4 provides a summary of the analysis from each case study, describing how leaders selectively looked at history to determine how to fight a contemporary adversary. Previous successes and failures acted as "anchors," drawing leaders' attention to specific events. These anchors biased leaders to look for, and assign more value to, information that confirmed their position. The synopsis moves from individual to organizational biases, evaluating the presence of groupthink in each case to determine its contribution in solidifying a leader's preconceived advocacy for a doctrine or concept.

Chapter 5 provides recommendations for organizations, individuals, and doctrine. Organizationally, it offers guidelines for institutionalizing a culture of adaptability to navigate today's strategic environment. Individually, it stresses the need for developing mental flexibility and the importance of understanding the assumptions of doctrine. Doctrinally, it suggests introducing more collaborative tools to produce broader operational solutions. Each area stresses the importance of keeping historical analysis in context and recommends methods to guard against individual and group cognitive biases.

How to guard against "the next great idea" is about reminding senior leaders to evaluate problems objectively, challenge assumptions constantly, and provide internalized criteria with which to assess possible solutions. These skills translate into a "peacetime equivalent of *coup d'oeil*, the ability to see, almost at a glance, which methods of future warfare have the best chance of working well in the context of only dimly foreseen circumstances and, perhaps even more important, *which methods do not*."[3]

---

[3] Harry R. Winton and David R. Mets, eds., foreward to *The Challenge of Change – Military Institutions and New Realities, 1918-1941* (Lincoln, NB: University of Nebraska Press, 2000), xv.

CHAPTER ONE: THEORETICAL FOUNDATIONS

This chapter provides the theoretical framework for the thesis. The first part defines doctrine, concept, and dogma and describes the relationship between doctrine and strategy. The chapter then shifts to describe decision errors, focusing on two cognition biases—"anchoring" and "confirmation bias"—and their potential to increase the occurrence of groupthink, an organizational pathology. Each case study will conclude with an analysis of defense leaders against these pitfalls to determine if cognitive biases and/or groupthink affected their decisions, causing them to embrace inappropriate doctrine or unproven concepts.

Defining Doctrine, Concept, and Dogma

Doctrine is "a generalization of what works best in a given situation." From this definition, one can infer that repeated instances of a situation will produce similar results if practitioners adhere to the doctrine's underlying logic. Doctrine provides a tempered analysis of experience and serves as a reference point used to guide strategy and action. Its abstract nature provides the foundation—not the definitive solution—upon which practitioners can base their decisions. Simply put, doctrine reflects the judgments of senior leaders about what "is" and "is not" possible from a military standpoint.[1]

The iterative nature of doctrine poses unique challenges to writers as they develop and draft it. Doctrine results primarily from the close examination of combat experience.[2] Additionally, the evolution of armed conflict demands that doctrine must also evolve to stay relevant. Doctrine is not just the product of hard-won experience in

---

[1] Barry A. Rosen, *The Sources of Military Doctrine* (Ithaca, NY: Cornell University Press, 1984), 14.

[2] Ibid., 169.

the heat of battle; the key to developing sound doctrine is objective analysis and an accurate interpretation of these experiences. Besides the difficulty in maintaining objectivity, doctrine must also evolve to stay current and relevant. This reality represents another challenge to doctrine writers, who must evaluate developments in technology and new concepts to determine if they necessitate a change to existing doctrine. Equally important, doctrine writers must reexamine the underlying assumptions of doctrinal precepts frequently. In some cases, a change to these assumptions may render the entire doctrine obsolete.[3] In most cases, though, one doctrine is never replaced in its entirety with another one. While some elements of doctrine are fleeting and replaced with new concepts and technologies, other elements are more resilient, reinventing themselves in newer forms. Whether a concept is evolutionary or revolutionary, it must be validated before earning the imprimatur of sanctioned doctrine. Even then, this distinction is not a guarantor of success; the real measure is "do we read it, do we understand it, do we use it, and does it work?"[4]

Since the introduction of new concepts is important to keeping doctrine relevant, it is necessary to distinguish the two terms. A concept springs from an inference based upon facts, suggesting that a pattern of behavior *may possibly* lead to a desired result; doctrine suggests that a pattern of behavior *will probably* lead to a desired result.[5] Two

---

[3] The development of airpower doctrine is illustrative. The success of long-range bombing in World War II and the advent of nuclear weapons reinforced the belief that strategic bombing would be decisive. This assumed all U.S. wars would be unlimited against industrialized nations. The Vietnam War, a limited war against a third-world adversary, invalidated the underlying assumptions of this doctrine. The resultant bombing campaign proved ineffective and indecisive. See Mark Clodfelter, *The Limits of Airpower – The American Bombing of North Vietnam* (Lincoln, NB: University of Nebraska Press, 2006).

[4] General Ronald Keys to Air Force Doctrine Symposium in 1997, quoted in U.S. Department of the Air Force, *Air Force Basic Doctrine, Organization, and Command, Air Force Doctrine Document 1* (Montgomery, AL: Lemay Center for Doctrine Development and Education, October 14 2011), 1.

[5] Irving B. Holley, *Technology and Military Doctrine* (Montgomery, AL: Air University Press, 2004), 21. Both concept and doctrine contain graduated degrees of certainty in achieving future success, implying a degree of uncertainty—we can never be completely sure. The Heisenberg Principle challenges

observations emerge from this distinction. First, practitioners should never regard doctrine as an absolute—following it mechanically does not assure success. Second, concepts must be tested to confirm or refute them; to espouse a concept as authoritative on inadequate grounds is dogma. Concepts that are tested and found to withstand the rigors of combat experience lead to generalizations, which may, in turn, become doctrine.

Relationship Between Doctrine and Strategy

Doctrine is the building material for strategy and is fundamental to sound judgment.[6] This observation highlights the relationship between doctrine and strategy. However, this relationship is not sacrosanct. The conventional political-military relationship invites views from policy makers, military leaders, and defense experts who possess a range of opinions concerning doctrine and strategy and their links to war and statecraft. These perspectives may explain the inclination to merge proven doctrine with untested concepts and technologies. The decision to include or discard new technology or concepts poses a continuing problem to even the most seasoned military professional.

The fact that leaders do not always give doctrine its due influence in strategy underscores another role of doctrine: serving as an introspective tool for analyzing its own success or failure in support of a strategy, in the process measuring not only its impact on the strategy decision process, but also its relevance. If leaders adhere to a certain doctrine, but fail to achieve their objectives, this failure should cause strategists to

---

the idea that we can accurately study any phenomenon (including historical events) absolutely. There are many instances where we can only approximate what it real. This validates the common historian refrain of "keeping things in context." See Jan Hilgevoord, "The Uncertainty Principle for Energy and Time," *American Journal of Physics* 64, no. 12 (December 1996), http://www.stat.physik.uni-potsdam.de/~pikovsky/teaching/ stud seminar/ajp uncert energy time1.pdf (referenced February 27, 2012).

[6] U.S. Department of the Air Force, *Air Force Doctrine Document 1*, 1.

reevaluate the doctrine. Likewise, if a strategy, informed by doctrine, successfully

achieves the objectives, this success should reinforce the soundness of that doctrine.[7]

Decision Making Theory and Decision Errors

The process of how humans assimilate information and make decisions continues

to be the subject of active research. Some decisions allow an individual the time to

research and process all information relevant to that decision; typically, though, time is a

factor, driving a balance between the time allotted to make a decision and the ability to

gather and evaluate enough information to make a decision accurately. In such cases

where time is a constraint, the human mind uses "heuristics," mental shortcuts that help

an individual reach a decision. According to psychologists Daniel Kahneman and Amos

Tversky, heuristics can contain cognitive biases that distort the perception of reality and

lure individuals into making bad decisions.[8] At times, these biases lead to rigid mental

frameworks "in which people approach and solve problems based on preconceived

notions and preset patterns of thought."[9] Among the biases identified in social science,

two emerge as most relevant to the military: "anchoring" and "confirmation bias."

"Anchoring" is the overreliance on specific information from the past to influence

a present or future decision. An anchor is a preconception that requires no authoritative

support to be believed. An individual sets an anchor on select information, unknowingly

establishing a bias for the interpretation of all other evidence relative to this anchored

information.[10] Prototyping, where individuals categorize and refine ideas to pick a "best

example," acts powerfully to influence the selection of an anchor. The tendency for

---

[7] Dennis Drew and Don Snow, "Military Doctrine" in *Making Strategy, An Introduction to National Security Processes and Problems* (Montgomery, AL: Air University Press, 1988), 174.
[8] Kahneman and Tversky, "Judgment under Uncertainty," 1127.
[9] Zachary Shore, *Blunder: Why Smart People Make Bad Decisions* (New York: Bloomsbury, 2008), 6.
[10] Kahneman and Tversky, "Judgment under Uncertainty,"1128.

7

humans to think in prototypes and metaphors could result in judgment error, for while the prototype fits an individual's perception of the best example for one situation, it may be irrelevant in another.[11] When forecasting the future, "people often use the past as the starting point, [and] while the past may be relevant, the environment may offer other pertinent clues to the future."[12] Placing too much focus on one aspect of the past may produce a flawed decision in present or future events.

Similarly, "confirmation bias" is the tendency to seek and assign more value to evidence that proves a belief or assumption, while ignoring or assigning less importance to evidence that would disprove it.[13] Studies demonstrate that individuals place increased value on information supporting their position because confirmatory information is "easier to deal with" cognitively than information that opposes their position.[14] It is easier for the mind to *see* a piece of information that supports, rather than opposes, a pre-established belief. Confirmation bias can occur anywhere in the decision process: in how an individual searches, interprets, or recalls information from memory.

First, individuals tend to search for evidence consistent with a position they already have rather than sifting through all relevant evidence, in effect confirming their existing beliefs.[15] Second, individuals may set higher standards for considering

---

[11] Understanding how we categorize and sort ideas and concepts helps explain how we reason. Categories are not arbitrary constructions of order, they show gradients of membership, where some members are better examples than others. Shore, *Blunder*, 102-104.

[12] Richard E. Kopelman and Anne L. Davis, "A Demonstration of the Anchoring Effect," The Decision Sciences Journal of Innovative Education, http://kelley.iupui.edu/dsjie/ Tips/ kopelman htm (accessed February 21, 2012).

[13] Jonathan St. B.T. Evans, *Bias in Human Reasoning: Causes and Consequence* (Hillsdale, NJ: Lawrence Erlbaum Associates, 1989), 41.

[14] Thomas Gilovich, *How We Know What Isn't So: The Fallibility of Human Reason in Everyday Life* (New York: The Free Press, 1991), 31.

[15] Ibid., 45.

information that opposes their preconceptions, biasing how they interpret information.[16] Finally, individuals may recall information selectively to reinforce a preconceived position, leading to rigid adherence to a belief despite evidence independent of its veracity.[17] In war planning, a leader's belief that a doctrine always delivers a desired result may result in ignoring evidence that the doctrine is inaccurate or inapplicable to the situation. Cognition biases confine an individual's knowledge of a subject matter. In turn, this limited perspective restricts an individual's objectivity within a group and potentially exposes them to "groupthink" pathologies.

Introduced by Irving L. Janis in 1972, groupthink is a mode of decision-making by a highly cohesive group that values group consensus more than decision accuracy.[18] The groupthink model (Figure 1) illustrates Janis' theory, including antecedent conditions, symptoms, and consequences. The model shows that the interaction of a cohesiveness group (Box A) with structural faults (Box B-1) and a provocative context (Box B-2) increases the likelihood of groupthink symptoms to develop. These symptoms (Box C) reflect the tendency of a group to display the characteristics of defective decision-making (Box D), ultimately resulting in the low probability of reaching a good decision.[19] In Chapter 5, each case study will be scored and tabulated with respect to groupthink antecedents and symptoms, enabling a quantitative analysis of the role of groupthink in the decision process that produced a flawed war strategy.

---

[16] Charles S. Taber and Milton Lodge, "Motivated Skepticism in the Evaluation of Political Beliefs", *American Journal of Political Science,* 50, no. 3 (July 2006): 757, under "confirmation bias in political beliefs," http://www.unc.edu/~fbaum/teaching/POLI891_Sp11/articles/AJPS-2006-Taber.pdf (accessed February 21, 2012).

[17] Evans, *Bias in Human Reasoning,* 82.

[18] Janis, *Groupthink,* 9.

[19] Ibid., 135.

The first two symptoms (C1.1, C1.2) reflect overconfidence in the group's abilities—the group believes its decisions will be morally correct and rationalizes any negative fallout from a poor decision. The next two symptoms (C2.1, C2.2) reflect close-mindedness and the tendency to marginalize outsiders. The last four symptoms

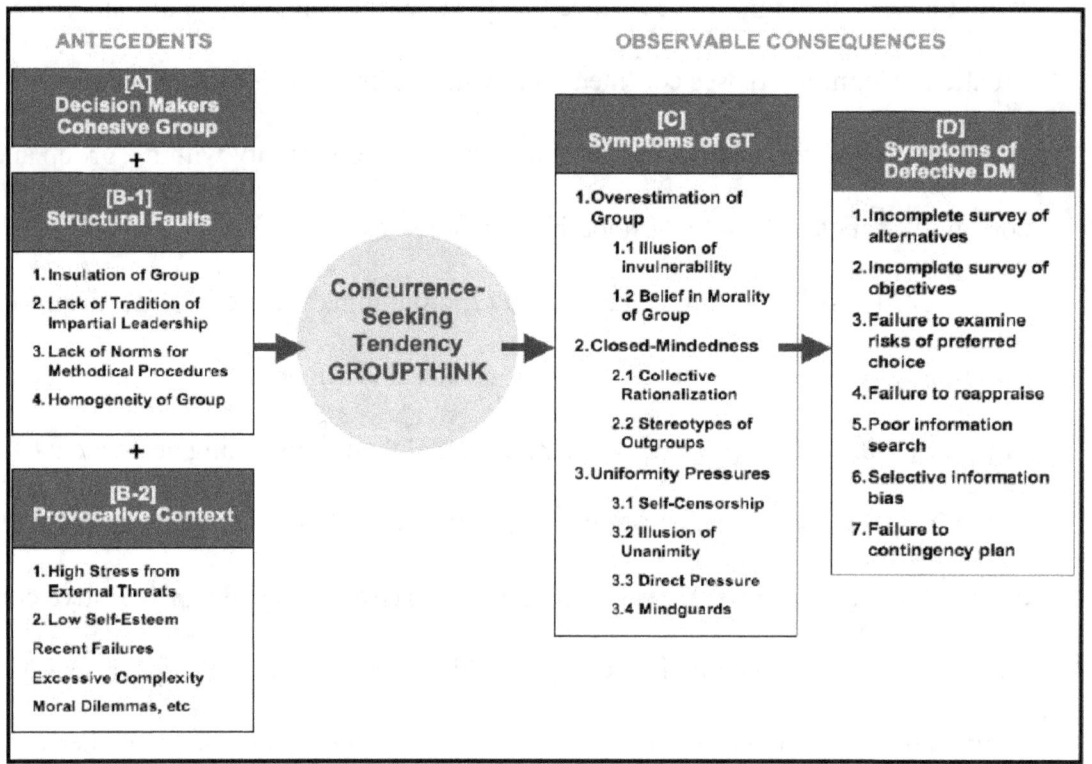

(C3.1–C3.4) pressure members to conform, limiting the inclusion of outside ideas.

Figure 1. Groupthink Theoretical Framework (adapted from Janis [1982], figure 10-1).[20]

All eight symptoms need not to be present for groupthink to occur, but probability does increase with evidence of more symptoms.[21] The occurrence of groupthink increases the *likelihood* of reaching a bad decision; it does not imply that a poor decision is *inevitable*.

---

[20] Chun Wei Choo, "Groupthink Theoretical Framework," University of Toronto, http://choo.fis.utoronto.ca/FIS/courses/lis2149/Groupthink.html (accessed April 9, 2012).

[21] David Ahlstrom and Linda C. Wang, "Groupthink and France's defeat in the 1940 campaign," *Journal of Management History* 15, no. 2 (2009): 162-163.

When a group experiences increased stress, members tend to marginalize key information and avoid decisions that could jeopardize group harmony. Stress also tends to accelerate the decision making process, leading to a condition where groups reach consensus too quickly, support the leader's preferred position, and focus almost entirely on information that confirms, rather than contradicts, the predominant position.[22] Such was the case in the French army in May 1940 on the eve of the Battle of France.

---

[22] Dieter Frey, Stefan Schulz-Hardt, and Dagmar Stahlberg "Information Seeking Among Individuals and Groups and Possible Consequences for Decision Making in Business and Politics" in *Understanding Group Behavior: Small Group Processes and Interpersonal Relations, Vol. 2* (Mahwah, NJ: Lawrence Erlbaum Associates, Inc., 1996), 211-212.

CHAPTER TWO: CASE STUDIES (DOCTRINE TO DOGMA)

This chapter presents two cases where leaders exhibited evidence of succumbing to individual and group cognitive biases, resulting in a dogmatic advocacy for doctrine inappropriate for the war they planned to fight. These intellectual shortfalls led to deviations from or rejections of more appropriate military doctrine, resulting in a delay or failure to meet strategic or military objectives. In the first case, the French Army's reliance on "the methodical battle" doctrine in World War II resulted in abject failure on the battlefield and the loss of the Republic. In the second narrative, the U.S. Army's pursuit of a "search and destroy" attrition strategy during the escalation period of the Vietnam War (1965-1968) resulted in thousands of American soldiers lost with no accompanying strategic success.

The Methodical Battle: The French Army in World War II

~ Preface ~

In the early hours of May 13, 1940, General Heinz Guderian's XIX Panzer Corps began crossing the Meuse River in Belgium, followed by a heavy aerial assault by the Luftwaffe. French Brigadier General Pierre Lafontaine should have directed his 55th Infantry Division to attack the bridgehead and halt the German advance, potentially changing the outcome of the Battle of Sedan. Per French doctrine, however, Lafontaine's location was too far to the rear, preventing him from obtaining a real-time picture of the situation. By the time intelligence filtered back to him, the conditions had changed, rendering Lafontaine's response incorrect for the "real" situation on the battlefield. Additionally, Lafontaine wasted precious hours looking for approval to attack from his superior, the commander of the French X Corps General Pierre-Paul Gransard. The lack of current intelligence and over-centralized control called for by methodical battle doctrine caused Lafontaine to delay the call for a counterattack.

Nine hours after the first Panzer crossed the Meuse and well after Lafontaine's subordinates would have preferred, he issued the order. The delay proved disastrous, giving Guderian's forces an invaluable head start to move across the river and secure a bridgehead. Allied attempts to bomb the Panzer Corps in the early hours of May 14 were ineffective in destroying the German bridgehead. Attacks by the heavier-armored French tanks later that morning met with success initially, but soon German attacks aided by the radio equipment in the Panzers enabled them to coordinate and mass forces more effectively, resulting in the destruction of the French armor. After this, the 55th Infantry Division ceased to function as a fighting force and retreated, enabling Guderian to break out from Sedan, streak across Belgium, and cut the Allies in two.[1]

When Germany launched its offensive against the Allies on May 10, 1940 to begin the Battle of France, no one on the Allied side predicted the ensuing route by the *Wehrmacht*. Confirming the Allied estimation of a lengthy campaign, British Prime Minister Winston Churchill assured President Franklin Delano Roosevelt, "I think myself the battle on land has only just begun."[2] Six weeks later, however, Germany had defeated the armies of France, Great Britain, Belgium, and the Netherlands; France sued for peace on June 22, 1940, signaling the historic collapse of the Third Republic.

---

[1] Peter R. Mansoor, "The Second Battle of Sedan, May 1940," *Military Review* 68 (June 1988): 64-75, http://cgsc.cdmhost.com/cdm/singleitem/collection/p124201coll1/id/514/rec/2704 (accessed January 7, 2012); Robert A. Doughty, *The Breaking Point: Sedan and the Fall of France, 1940* (Hamden, CT: Archon Books, 1990), 97-99.

[2] Warren F. Kimball, ed., *Churchill and Roosevelt: The Complete Correspondence* (Princeton, NJ: Princeton University Press, 1984), vol. 1, 37, quoted in Eliot S. Cohen and John Gooch, *Military Misfortunes – The Anatomy of Failure in War* (New York: The Free Press, 1990), 197.

The French army's resolute defeat necessitates a closer examination of the battle plan and the underlying doctrine that informed it. Wartime testimony confirms this, as French soldiers repeatedly "criticized what they perceived as the inherent weakness in the army's doctrine."[3] The French Army's own official history offers that while the army was prepared to mobilize, it was not ready for the mobile warfare it encountered in 1940... it was not "ready for combat."[4] Robert Doughty, a Professor of History at the United States Military Academy, summarizes the reality of *le Grande Armeé*:

> The French army, in short, had formulated a doctrine, organized and equipped its units, and trained its soldiers for the wrong type of war. The framework for this doctrine, and thus for the organization, equipment, training, and employment of French units, came from an emphasis on the destructiveness of firepower, the strength of the defense, the ascendancy of methodical battle, and the unifying power of the commander.[5]

Doctrine and the concomitant elements of organizing, training, and equipping a force are fundamentally the obligation of military leadership. Thus, responsibility for France's defeat in the early stages of World War II lay primarily at the feet of the French High Command. Marc Bloch, a French historian who participated in the Battle of France, corroborates this assertion. "Whatever the deep-seated causes of the disaster may have been, the immediate occasion was the utter incompetence of the High Command."[6] French military leaders dogmatically adhered to their sanctioned doctrine of *bataille*

---

[3] Robert A. Doughty, *Seeds of Disaster: The Development of French Army Doctrine, 1919-1939* (Hamdon, CN: Archon Books, 1985), 3. The Riom Trial (February 1942 to May 1943) was an attempt by the Vichy France regime, headed by Marshal Pétain, to indict the leaders of the Third Republic as responsible for France's defeat in 1940. The trial did not go as planned, as defendants rebutted the charges levied against them and demonstrated that failures of the French general staff under Pétain ultimately resulted in defeat.

[4] France, Ministere de la defense, Etat-major de l; armeé terre, Service historique, Lt Col Henry Dutailly, *Les Problems de l' armeé de terre francaise (1935-1939)* (Paris: Imprimerie nationale, 1980), 289, quoted in Doughty, *Seeds of Disaster, 3.*

[5] Ibid.

[6] Marc Bloch, *Strange Defeat*, trans. Gerard Hopkins (New York: Octagon Books, 1968), 25.

conduit (the methodical battle) in the Battle of France. This adherence to the limits

imposed by the rigid doctrine resulted in the quick surrender of the French State in 1940.

Years earlier, then Major Charles de Gaulle lamented a French army that "became

stuck in a set of ideas which had had their heyday before the end of the previous war."[7]

The French high command's intellectual rut provides an unremitting example of how

dogmatic adherence to inappropriate—and in this case, outdated—doctrine can lead to

devastating defeat. It becomes important, then, to look not only at the events of 1940, but

also at the preceding 20 years of French military history to analyze the evolution of the

methodical battle and its influence on French strategy entering World War II.

~ Evolution of the Methodical Battle ~

Methodical battle originated in 1918 during the Allied campaigns of World War I,

when the Allies finally overcame the stagnation of trench warfare on the Western Front.

From 1915 to 1917, Allied forces attempted several offensives designed to breakthrough

Axis lines, but each met with absolute failure. Heavily influenced by French military

theorist Ardant du Picq's emphasis on the moral and psychological aspects of battle,

Colonel Louis de Grandmaison's *offensive à outrance* sentenced legions of soldiers to

their deaths in spirited, but ill-fated charges into the teeth of German machine guns.[8] The

loss of nearly one million soldiers took its toll on the French Army, which mutinied after

another costly fight at the Second Battle of Aisne in May 1917. The impact of nearly

30,000 soldiers leaving the front lines to rear positions shocked French leaders into the

realization that élan was not enough to win the day.[9]

---

[7] Charles de Gaulle, *War Memoris, Volume I: The Call to Honour 1940-1942* (London: Weidenfeld & Nicolson, 1955), 13, quoted in Cohen and Gooch, 200.
[8] Doughty, *Seeds of Disaster*, 73.
[9] Martin Gilbert, *The First World War: A Complete History* (New York: Henry Holt and Co., 1994), 333.

The French abandoned these reckless assaults and developed tactics that met with better success: carefully coordinated offensives accompanied by massive artillery firepower. Marshal Philippe Pétain's attack at La Malmaison from October 23 to November 2, 1917 and General Marie-Eugène Debeney's advance at Montdidier on August 8, 1918 to start the Hundred Days Offensive offered textbook examples of how the methodical battle minimized French casualties, secured victory, and helped end the war.[10] Once the conflict ended in November 1918, the French Army looked to codify this measured approach into its doctrine during the interwar years.

On the battlefield, methodical battle stipulated that forces marshal and employ according to strict timetables and phase lines. Before an attack commenced, the commander ensured all forces were in place: armor, artillery, and air forces all synchronized in support of the infantry. After the infantry attacked and moved to the outer limits of armor and artillery supporting fires, it halted the advance to enable its support fires to redeploy and adjust their coverage. With support fires reestablished, the infantry offensive would proceed. The methodical advance of forces required centralized control at the highest levels of French command.[11] Such a restrictive advance flowed as the natural byproduct of an overwhelming focus on defense, with forces deploying from established defensive positions to mount a coordinated offensive.

In formulating this doctrine, the French recognized the primacy of firepower on the modern battlefield. *"Le feu tue"* became the catchphrase of a force focused on this

---

[10] Ibid., 369, 410. Montdidier demonstrated the three central tenets of the French offensive: the first, rigid centralized control, facilitated the other two – supporting an infantry attack with massive artillery and dividing an offensive operation into a series of smaller efforts rather than an "all out" thrust. Eugenia C. Kiesling, *Arming Against Hitler: France and the Limits of Military Planning* (Lawrence, KS: University of Kansas Press, 1996), 140.
[11] Doughty, *Seeds of Disaster*, 4.

element of modern war.[12] The French Army's emphasis on firepower does not imply that it focused solely on the defense; constant tension between offense and defense dominated French military discourse during the interwar years. Still, the devastating lethality of modern firepower meant that offensives required materiel superiority—a constant challenge for France against its neighbor across the Rhine. Ultimately, Germany's steady rearmament and fortification of the border, combined with French national policy to reduce its conscription term to one year, tilted French doctrine toward the defense.[13]

The ascendency of firepower in French doctrine was not in isolation; advances in motorization and mechanization in the 1920s and 1930s spawned widespread innovation within the French army. General Jean Baptiste Eugène Estienne, father of the French "tank" arm, urged that armor evolve into an independent branch separate from the infantry; he deemed it essential that tanks remain in general reserve and not assigned organically to an infantry division.[14] Likewise, de Gaulle's *Towards the Professional Army* proposed a 100,000-man army of professional "armored" soldiers. To a nation steeped in the republican tradition of the citizen-soldier, de Gaulle's advocacy for a large standing army was threatening to the aristocracy: his "aggressive weapons" could start an offensive war with Germany or support a military *coup d' etat* against the French polity.[15]

Unfortunately, Pétain and the general staff failed to realize the newfound ability of a motorized and mechanized force to achieve a rapid breakthrough of a defensive

---

[12] First coined by Pétain, *le feu tue*, or "fire kills," became a truism repeated piously by practically every French writer to emphasize the killing power of artillery. Doughty, *Seeds of Disaster*, 74.

[13] Soon after this policy went into effect, French readiness along the border plummeted from twelve to six full-ready divisions. The one-year conscript term incentivized a shift to defensive tactics and construction of the Maginot Line. Rosen, *The Sources of Military Doctrine*, 108.

[14] With his forced retirement in 1927, General Estienne's concepts for tank employment on the battlefield were never integrated into French doctrine. Brian Bond and Martin Alexander, "Liddell Hart and De Gaulle: The Doctrines of Limited Liability and Mobile Defense" in *Makers of Modern Strategy from Machiavelli to the Nuclear Age,* eds. Peter Paret, Gordon A. Craig, and Felix Gilbert (Princeton, NJ: Princeton University Press, 1986), 599-604.

[15] Ibid., 613-617.

position not just to infiltrate the enemy line, but also to slice off major segments of an established front.[16] Most new weapons were "grafted" onto old tactics, and despite the introduction of motorized vehicles onto the battlefield, the infantry remained the "queen of battle" charged with the principal mission in combat. "Preceded, protected, and accompanied by the fires of artillery, aided eventually by combat tanks and aviation, it conquers, occupies, organizes, and secures the terrain."[17] Despite new equipment, French doctrine in the 1930s had "regressed [as] notions of the methodical battle and firepower dominated the methods for employing new weaponry."[18]

~ French Army Strategy in the Battle of France ~

It is at this point that methodical battle doctrine and the French war plan start to merge. The bulk of natural resources and French industry were in proximity to the Rhineland and thus vulnerable to a German attack, posing a considerable strategic challenge to French leaders. Indeed, the Rhineland's inherent vulnerability "contributed to France's adoption of a strategy emphasizing defense of this crucial war-making capability."[19] To protect its frontier, France relied on a combination of defensive fortifications, natural terrain, and a network of trenches and bunkers along its northeastern border. Combined with a French aversion to fighting on their soil, the

---

[16] Doughty, *Seeds of Disaster*, 108-109. France's premier tank, the Char B1, illustrates the limited role French leaders envisioned for armor. The B1 was conceived to breakthrough a defensive line, with large treads to navigate over trenches. Since it was tied to the infantry, it lacked speed relative to German armor, restricting its tactical mobility. Likewise, its high fuel consumption limited its strategic mobility. Steve Zaloga, *Panzer IV vs Char B1 Bis: France 1940* (Oxford, England: Osprey Pub, 2011), 8-11.

[17] France, Ministere de la guerre, *Instruction provisoire sur l'emploi tactique des grandes unites* (Paris: Charles Lavauzelle, 1922), 23, quoted in Robert A. Doughty, "The Evolution of French Military Doctrine" (master's thesis, Army Command and General Staff College, 1976), 45, http://www.scribd.com/doc/8033074/Evolution-of-French-Army-Doctrine-19191939 (accessed January 14, 2012).

[18] Doughty, *Seeds of Disaster*, 181-182.

[19] World War I highlighted the importance of protecting France's natural resources. Coal, steel, lead ore, and iron ore production dropped substantially from 1913-1915, after German occupation. Following World War I, practitioners expected modern weapons to demand more raw materials, exacerbating France's vulnerability. Ibid., 41.

18

requirement to defend the French frontier relied on channeling any German offensive north of the Ardennes Forest, out of France and into Belgium.[20] Thus, the French High Command proposed and constructed the Maginot Line along its northeastern border "to canalize the Germans toward the northern frontier [and] permit the concentration and movement of large French forces into Belgium."[21]

The war plan relied on deploying French troops to the Dyle River in Belgium to establish defensive positions. Unfortunately for France, Belgium declared neutrality in 1936, preventing the French from pre-deploying forward once Germany invaded Poland in 1939. At this point, either the assumptions in the French war plan or the doctrine of methodical battle doctrine needed to change. The commander in chief of Allied forces, French General Maurice Gamelin, did neither. In November 1939 and again in March 1940, he proposed shifting forces from the Allied right and center to link up with Belgian and Dutch forces and strengthen the left flank. This required a deeper movement across Belgium into the Netherlands, stretching the Allied line and relying on reserve forces to deploy north. General Alphonse Joseph Georges, Gamelin's commander of land forces, protested against committing the major part of Allied reserves that far north to respond to German action that could amount to nothing more than a diversion.[22]

When the Battle of France started on May 10, 1940, Georges' spirited dissent proved prescient. As hostilities began, the Allied line was strong on the left and right, but weak in the center, opposite the Ardennes Forest, particularly in the Sedan sector. Although the initial German attack did advance across northern Belgium and the

---

[20] In the event of a German attack, the French planned to establish a defensive line that would keep the battle away from French territory and industry. German violation of Belgian territory would bring Britain into the war, since security of Flemish ports was a concern of the British Navy. Rosen, *The Sources of Military Doctrine*, 114.

[21] Doughty, *Seeds of Disaster*, 67.

[22] Cohen and Gooch, *Military Misfortunes*, 202.

Netherlands, the Germans used this secondary effort to divert attention from their main effort through the Ardennes Forest. Still, the Germans pushed the Dutch and Belgian armies on the Allied left without difficulty. As French reserves committed north to reinforce retreating Dutch and Belgian forces, the main thrust of German forces carved its way through the Ardennes Forest and crossed the Meuse River at Sedan on May 13, 1940. Following the Dutch surrender on May 14, 1940, French reserve forces redeployed back into Belgium, but were unable to set up a defensive reserve. Guderian's Panzers had already broken a 50-mile gap in the Allied front.[23]

Charging to the English Channel, Guderian's Panzer Corps cut the Allied forces in two, leading to the rapid end of hostilities in the Low Countries on May 28, 1940. As the battle moved into France, German forces routed the French, forcing the French army to retreat south to avoid encirclement and annihilation. German mechanized forces pierced the Maginot Line to the east, causing the remaining French armies to retreat further south as the German Army advanced on all fronts. On June 22, 1940, France and Germany signed an armistice. The Germans defeated the French Army a mere six weeks after first contact and helped install the Vichy government.[24]

~ Anchoring and Confirmation Bias ~

As the general staff prepared for possible war, the huge losses and deep emotions of World War I formed an immutable bond between past experiences and preparations for the "next war." Criticizing how the army selectively applied lessons from the Franco-Prussia War from (1870-71) in anticipation of war in 1914, the general staff asserted they would not repeat this error—they would learn the "correct" lessons this time. They

---

[23] Ibid., 202-203.
[24] Ibid., 203-206.

anchored on firepower, using battles at La Malmaison in October 1917 and Montdidier in August 1918 as textbook examples to highlight the role of firepower in the methodical battle. La Malmaison became "the model for attacks with limited objectives."

Likewise, Montdidier became the single-source reference for the methodical battle, providing students "a clear model of a relatively mobile attack against an enemy in prepared defensive positions."[25] The leaders of these battles, Pétain and Debeney, gave credibility to the elevated status of these battles in French lore. Pétain, appointed Marshal of France in 1918, forever maintained that artillery embodied his conviction "firepower kills." Likewise, as commandant of the French War College, Debeney influenced the legend surrounding that "black day" of the war for Germany.

These battles stood atop the mound of France's limited success, seemingly daring the High Command to look elsewhere for object lessons. The success of Pétain's forces in the first major action after the 1917 mutiny blinded the general staff to problems with counter-battery fire and the difficulty of coordinating between infantry and artillery units at La Malmaison. Likewise, instructors reveled at the glory of Montdidier as the "turning point" of the war, painting the German adversary as a static foe unable to match France's brilliant new tactics.[26] In both battles, powerful emotions lashed onto the more clinical cognitive realization that the French won due to focused and massive firepower.

If anchoring on firepower at La Malmaison and Montdidier biased the general staff in its vision of future war, confirmation bias prevented them from preparing for it.

---

[25] The Battle of La Malmaison was an emotionally significant battle in French army lore. The French changed their doctrine and mounted a successful offensive, reclaiming the ridge at Chemin des Dames – the same site where, five months earlier, horrific losses under Robert Nivelle led to widespread mutinies across the French army. Likewise, the Battle of Montdidier represented a resounding victory largely independent of American aid, a glorious and important achievement for the French. Doughty, *Seeds of Disaster*, 81-83.

[26] Ibid., 82.

This bias kept the general staff from incorporating mechanization and motorization into their operational concepts, as they failed to realize the advantages of maneuverability on the battlefield offered by a motorized force.[27] Lacking imagination, the French focused weapons development on attrition-style warfare and limited employment concepts to the pedantic speed of the infantry, always the centerpiece of the methodical battle.[28] Insidiously, confirmation bias caused the staff to recall the lessons from La Malmaison and Montdidier selectively, reinforcing their preconceived notions of war in the future and limiting the adoption of new concepts.

Leaders scrutinized battles from World War I and the Spanish Civil War, and the absence of countervailing lessons reassured them of the soundness of their doctrine rather than casting doubts on it. Methodical battle, by all accounts, was an enduring doctrine that withstood the test of conflict. Ironically, France's leaders committed the same error they had accused their predecessors of in 1914, anchoring on select historical experiences and basing the entirety of their doctrine on a limited view of past events.

~ Groupthink ~

Evidence of the first antecedent, "group cohesiveness," is abundant among senior leaders in the French general staff during the interwar years. Among other decorated World War I veterans, Pétain and Gamelin remained in the service late in life and served in influential positions rather than passing responsibility to the next generation, cutting off all new ideas for how to fight.[29] These seasoned veterans rose to become the military Commanders-in-Chief, wielding tremendous influence with respect to French policy,

---

[27] Ibid., 108-109.
[28] Doughty, "The Evolution of French Military Doctrine," 45.
[29] Ahlstrom and Wang, "Groupthink and France's defeat in the 1940 campaign," 167.

training, and doctrine. The terrors of World War I bound this inner circle of leaders into a highly cohesive group, creating a culture of like-mindedness anchored on firepower.

The homogeneity of the group illustrates the second antecedent condition, "organizational structural faults." The general staff's unified position on the methodical battle is a natural byproduct of the group's cohesion and reflects a "normalization" of their viewpoints. Populated with graduates of the French War College and its focus on La Malmaison and Montdidier, the general staff all praised the methodical battle as the chosen doctrine.[30] Tanks and aircraft were ruled out as maneuver arms, radios and communications were neglected, and decentralized control was never tested—in short, uniformity, not ingenuity, became the currency of the French army after World War I.[31]

The third antecedent, a "provocative situational context," is evident in the high stress created by an external threat (Germany) with low hope of finding a solution other than the leader's favored position—in this case, Gamelin's employment of the methodical battle despite reports on German tactics in Poland that rendered the doctrine obsolete.[32] "Solidarity increases markedly whenever a collection of individuals faces a common source of external stress."[33] For twenty years, the general staff rejected other methods to fight the next war. When finally faced with that war, it was too late to change—the French had to fight with the tactically limited army they developed, trained, and fielded.

These antecedents enabled groupthink symptoms to develop in the French general staff. The first symptoms concern an overestimation of the group's abilities, specifically a "belief in the inherent morality of the group." The anguish of 5,600,000 casualties in

---

[30] Doughty, *Seeds of Disaster*, 82-83.
[31] Ibid., 4.
[32] Kiesling, *Arming Against Hitler*, 170.
[33] Janis, *Groupthink*, 5.

World War I presented a strong moral imperative for the general staff to avoid mass casualties in the next war and impacted their decision to pursue a defensive doctrine. They could not help but remember the low moral point of the war, when soldiers mutinied against Neville in April 1917. The staff understood that flawed doctrine led to the slaughter of thousands and were confident the methodical battle would prevent a repeat disaster. General Debeney led a chorus of like-minded leaders focused on the defense, co-authoring the 1921 *Provisional Instructions on the Tactical Employment of Large Units,* which prescribed *bataille conduit* (methodical battle) as French doctrine.[34]

The second set of symptoms, "close-mindedness," includes efforts to discount warnings that may lead members to reconsider their assumptions.[35] The general staff's exploitation of Pétain and Gamelin's scarce understanding of airpower in French doctrine is illustrative. While both leaders were knowledgeable about ground forces, neither understood aircraft capabilities; the air arm, and entire French Army, suffered from this naïvety.[36] Real-world events did not overcome this ignorance, as the general staff suppressed urgent reports from Poland on German success at coordinating air and ground forces, preventing a much-needed re-evaluation of French doctrine.[37]

The third set of groupthink symptoms, "pressure towards uniformity," includes self-censorship, a shared illusion of unanimity, and direct pressure on members who express dissent.[38] The general staff's use of "direct pressure on dissenters" prevented the consideration of other operational concepts. While acknowledging the value of tanks and

---

[34] Doughty, *Seeds of Disaster,* 6.

[35] Janis, *Groupthink,* 198.

[36] James S. Corum, "A Clash of Military Cultures: German and French Approaches to Technology Between the World Wars" (paper presented at the USAF Academy Symposium, Colorado Springs, CO, September 1994), 35-36, http://www.au.af.mil/au/awc/awcgate/saas/corum.pdf (accessed March 4, 2012).

[37] Ahlstrom and Wang, "Groupthink and France's Defeat in the 1940 Campaign," 173.

[38] Janis, *Groupthink,* 198.

aircraft as technological achievements, the staff failed to appreciate both elements as maneuver arms, requiring a paradigm shift from attrition-style warfare. Offering dissent, General Estienne, father of the French "tank" arm and Major Charles De Gaulle argued that armor should not be tethered to infantry, but should form into autonomous units. In response, leaders forced Estienne to retire early and delayed de Gaulle's promotion to Colonel, arguing that the Germans would find French forces stronger and more doctrinally sound than the army the Germans encountered in Poland in 1939.[39]

While geography and circumstances found critical portions of French industry and natural resources strategically vulnerable; and post-World War I demographics, in part, drove the French to base their military forces on lesser-trained reservists, the proximate cause of French defeat in 1940 was the general staff's dogmatic reliance on the doctrine of the methodical battle. Individual and group cognitive biases contributed to this misplaced confidence by defense leaders, but as the next case study will illustrate, the French Army was not alone in succumbing to these mental errors.

---

[39] Bond and Alexander, "The Doctrines of Limited Liability and Mobile Defense," 603-604; Ahlstrom and Wang, "Groupthink and France's Defeat in the 1940 Campaign," 169-170.

Search and Destroy: The U.S. Army in Vietnam

~ Preface ~

In the summer of 1965, President Lyndon B. Johnson made an open-ended commitment to defend the Republic of Vietnam (RVN). Johnson's pledge resulted from the growing crisis that left a beleaguered RVN government and military on the verge of collapse and defeat by the communist insurgency. The limited application of U.S. power, including an intermittent bombing campaign, had failed in its endeavor to stop North Vietnam's support of the Viet Cong. U.S. officials recognized the insurgency required a larger U.S. presence to prevent a communist takeover of the country.

Following the first U.S. action of the war in the Ia Drang Valley in November 1965, Colonel Hal Moore led his unit, the 3rd Brigade, 1st Cavalry Division, into Binh Din to sweep communist forces from the province. Immediately following a heavy artillery bombardment used to prepare a landing zone (LZ), Moore encountered a bewildered Vietnamese family in a nearby village. Huddled in their house, the parents were caring for their young daughter, who had been wounded by stray artillery fire. As Moore arranged for a medical evacuation, he was alarmed by what this said about the war. "It struck me that we were not in Vietnam to kill or maim innocent men and women and children and tear up their houses. We were there to find and kill the enemy."[40]

Americans referred to the area near Moore's encounter as LZ Dog, "just another spot to disgorge…search for and destroy the enemy." To the Vietnamese, though, the hamlet near Phung Du "was a place of history, identity, and a distinct soul."[41] Even though 3rd Brigade was trained in conventional war, they were in Vietnam to secure the

---

[40] John C. McManus. *Grunts: Inside the American Infantry Combat Experience, World War II Through Iraq* (New York: New American Library, 2010), 183-184.
[41] Ibid.

26

loyalty of the South Vietnamese, an objective more akin to counterinsurgency.[42] This thesis does not discuss whether Vietnam was "the wrong war – at the wrong place, at the wrong time, with the wrong enemy."[43] Rather, it analyzes the actions of senior leaders during the period of U.S. escalation from 1965-1968. Discounting years of knowledge on counterinsurgency (COIN) practices, Army leaders assumed that superior firepower, technology, and mobility would reduce communist forces and enable the U.S. to win in a war of attrition against the Viet Cong.

~ Evolution of U.S. Army Doctrine in the 1960s ~

More than any other factor, defense policy shaped Army doctrine, organization, and equipment heading into Vietnam. The bipolar paradigm of post-World War II compelled U.S. policy to concentrate on the "most dangerous" threat in Western Europe instead of the "most likely" threat: brushfires that constituted all U.S. engagements from World War II forward. U.S. experiences with civil war in Greece (1946-1949), the Huk rebellion in the Philippines (1949-1951), and an insurgency on the fringes of the Korean War (1948-1954) were deemed unique and relegated to the "special case" category.[44]

In 1962, the Army Field Manuals (FM) defined COIN doctrine in progressive levels of specificity. Cast as "counter-guerrilla operations," the 31-series of manuals outlined COIN as an extension of unconventional warfare. While FM 31-16 suggested "pacification" committees comprised of "military personnel and representatives from the civilian administrative and paramilitary agencies," it emphasized fighting like with like.[45] The insurgent was "to be fought with a mirror image of guerrilla tactics…a model

---

[42] Ibid.

[43] General Omar Bradley, quoted in Andrew Krepinevich, *The Army and Vietnam* (Baltimore, MD: Johns Hopkins University Press, 1986), 4.

[44] Krepinevich, foreward to *The Army and Vietnam*, xii.

[45] U.S. Department of the Army, *Counterguerrilla Operations,* FM 31-16 (Washington, DC: Department of the Army, February 1963), 38.

constructed from the U.S. Army's own experience in...offensive guerrilla warfare."[46]

This image did not reflect guerrilla warfare as espoused by Mao Tse Tung or the

Vietnamese, but rather the predilections of "American guerrilla" forces, including Special

Forces, paramilitary units, and indigenous recruits.[47] None of the 31-series manuals

mentioned winning "hearts and minds" or societal development.[48]

The surge in 31-series literature projected the appearance of an Army serious

about COIN, yet statements offered by senior leaders revealed the service's disinterest in

what it considered a "cloud of dust" from the Kennedy administration. This distinction

undermined the move by COIN doctrine from theory to practice, and sustained the

exalted status of conventional warfare.[49] Dismissing any "perceived" difference between

COIN (and its nation-building approach) and conventional warfare, General Earle G.

Weaver, Army Chief of Staff in 1962, asserted, "it is fashionable...to say that the

problems in Southeast Asia are primarily political and economic rather than military. I

do not agree. The essence of the problem in Vietnam is military."[50]

While Special Forces folded unconventional warfare into its COIN doctrine, "Big

Army" doctrine reflected the Army's tendency to fit all forms of conflict within the

familiar construct of conventional war.[51] The 1962 version of its "bible," FM-100,

discussed COIN for the first time, stating, " operations to suppress and eliminate irregular

---

[46] Michael Mclintock, *Instruments of Statecraft: U.S. Guerrilla Warfare, Counterinsurgency, and Counterterrorism, 1940-1990* (New York, NY: Pantheon Books, 1992), 217.

[47] Mao's "Protracted War" outlines a three-phase approach to seize political power within the state. It involves a Strategic Defensive phase, a Strategic Stalemate phase, and a Strategic Offensive phase. Maoist strategy does not require a sequential application of the three stages. For more, see Mao Tse-Tung, *On Guerrilla Warfare*, trans. Samuel B. Griffith (Urbana, IL: University of Illinois Press, 1961).

[48] Mclintock, *Instruments of Statecraft*, 217.

[49] U.S. Army General Maxwell Taylor, quoted in Krepinevich, *The Army and Vietnam*, 37.

[50] Roger Hilsman, *To Move a Nation* (Garden City, NY: Doubleday & Co., 1967), 426 quoted in Austin G. Long, *Doctrine of Eternal Recurrence: U.S. Military and Counterinsurgency Doctrine, 1960-1970 and 2003-2006* (Santa Monica, CA: RAND National Defense Research Institute, 2008), 9, http://www.rand.org/pubs/occasional_papers/2008/RAND_OP200.pdf (accessed November 10, 2011).

[51] Krepinevich, *The Army and Vietnam*, 39.

forces are primarily offensive in nature. Thus the conventional force must plan and seize the initiative at the outset."[52] By 1964, the Army had not yet published doctrine that addressed COIN at the Army level; its patchwork formulation reflected the activities of a service going through the motions to satisfy the requirements of civilian leadership.[53]

Assuming future war would resemble Europe in 1945, "Big Army" doctrine in the 1960's was a continuation of conventional warfare developed in World War II and refined later in Korea. The clichéd expression "send a bullet, not a man" encapsulated the Army's belief in firepower to secure victory on the contemporary battlefield. The emphasis on firepower, technology, and strategic mobility caused Army leadership to think conventional warfare and its underlying doctrine would apply evenly to all conflicts short of nuclear war, including limited wars and insurgencies.

The Army's focus on conventional warfare affected its work in advising the Army of the Republic of Vietnam (ARVN) from 1954-1965, during which time U.S. forces helped organize and train the South Vietnamese on doctrine deemed by some as too heavily weighted toward sweep-type operations and other conventional military tactics.[54] The familiarity of preparing for twenty years to fight the last war instead of the next one (and advising its key partner on the same methods) formed the foundation of the Army's approach as it entered the "fog-shrouded terrain of a people's war" in Vietnam.[55]

---

[52] U.S. Department of the Army, *Field Service Regulations, Operations,* FM 100-5 (Washington, DC: Department of the Army, 1962), 139.

[53] Krepinevich, *The Army and Vietnam*, 40.

[54] Maxwell Taylor, "Letter to President Kennedy," November 3, 1961, in U.S. Department of State, *Foreign Relations of the United States, 1961-1963, Vol I, Vietnam 1961* (Washington, DC: Government Printing Office, 1988) quoted in Long, *Doctrine of Eternal Recurrence*, 10.

[55] Krepinevich, foreward to *The Army and Vietnam*, xi.

~ U.S. Strategy in Vietnam: June 1965 to January 1968 ~

In June 1965, General William C. Westmoreland, Commander of Military Assistance Command Vietnam (MACV) notified the Joint Chiefs that the Viet Cong (VC) had moved to stage three of its insurgency, evidenced by its overrunning of ARVN forces at Binh Dinh.[56] VC forces had grown to the point that they posed an immediate threat to the RVN. Westmoreland was convinced the North would commit whatever forces necessary to topple the South. "If South Vietnam was to survive…the United States had to make an 'active commitment' with troops that could…take the war to the enemy."[57] Viewing these forces as a stopgap to save the ARVN, he requested an increase of 175,000 men to bolster U.S. forces and achieve a friendly to enemy force ratio of 3:1.[58]

Westmoreland's strategy involved three phases. Phase One employed forty-four battalions in a defensive posture to stem the advance of the VC, stabilize the situation, and provide the RVN time to reestablish its legitimacy by the end of 1965. Phase Two required twenty-four additional battalions in 1966 to seize the initiative by invading and eliminating VC sanctuaries. Phase Three moved to sustained combat, "mopping up" any remaining insurgents. Across all phases, the Army would pursue pacification and reinforce the ARVN.[59] This force posture enabled Westmoreland to employ an attrition strategy after the situation stabilized and MACV moved into Phase Two of its campaign.

---

[56] Not everyone agreed with Westmoreland's assessment. Under Secretary of State William C. Ball questioned the Army's fixation with Phase 3 insurgency warfare, stating this approach ignored the possibility that the VC, fighting a protracted war, might retire back to stage three operations instead of facing superior U.S. forces. Ibid., 156.

[57] William C. Westmoreland, *A Soldier Reports* (Garden City, NY: Doubleday & Co., Inc, 1976), 140.

[58] This differed from the traditional COIN force ratio of 10:1 used in colonial tactics; MACV constructed the 3:1 ratio assuming the U.S. advantage in firepower would mitigate any risk inherent in the lower ratio. Krepinevich, *The Army and Vietnam*, 157-159.

[59] Westmoreland, *A Soldier Reports*, 142, 145; Krepinevich, *The Army and Vietnam*, 166.

Westmoreland felt attrition was the only way to secure the population; "it was not enough merely to contain the big units. They had to be pounded with artillery and bombs [and] brought to battle."[60] Bringing the enemy to battle was critical to the strategy's success, so when the enemy refused to engage, the Army attempted "search and destroy" missions to chase and defeat the enemy on the run.[61] Despite ample evidence that ARVN search operations "failed to establish any contact with major VC units," U.S. units adopted the same "sweep" strategy.[62] Although the Army did catch VC forces in large battles, none of these fights amounted to a *decisive* battle.[63] Viet Cong forces were always able to slip away, reconstitute their forces, and recover lost ground.

The Army also engaged in cordon and search operations to "clear" a village of enemy resistance and destroy his support base. Clearing operations usually lasted longer than sweep operations and placed greater emphasis on pacification. Besides sweeps and clearing operations, the Army used "securing" operations to destroy the enemy's political infrastructure and protect the achievements of pacification. In theory, the proper sequence involved "search and destroy" operations to engage the enemy's main force, followed by "clear" and "secure" operations to displace any remaining enemy forces. In practice, though, commanders thought the main purpose of tactical operations was to

---

[60] Westmoreland, *A Soldier Reports*, 150.
[61] The Army replaced the term "search and destroy" with other, more gratifying terms, including combat sweep, spoiling attack, and reconnaissance in force. Robert A. Doughty, *The Evolution of U.S. Army Tactical Doctrine, 1946-1976* (Fort Leavenworth, KS: Combat Studies Institute, 1979), 31-32, http://usacac.army.mil/cac2/cgsc/carl/resources/csi/Doughty/doughty.asp (accessed October 11, 2012).
[62] MACV, Office of the Assistant Chief of Staff, Intelligence, "VC Tactics – Withdrawal," 18 March 1965, MHI, I, 16 quoted in Krepinevich, *The Army and Vietnam*, 167.
[63] Krepinevich, *The Army and Vietnam*, 167. One could argue the Tet Offensive in January 1968 was the decisive battle the U.S. was seeking. VC forces were never able to reconstitute after Tet, instead retreating to resume Phase Two operations until the end of the war. The battle also marked the turning point for U.S. political support, which declined rapidly following the battle.

"find, fix, fight, and finish" the enemy. Destroying the enemy assumed greater importance than the textbook sequence of "search and destroy," "clear," and "secure."[64]

The Battle of the Ia Drang Valley in November 1965 provided the first acid test for attrition strategy. While the battle validated the concept of air mobility to transport, concentrate, maneuver, or withdraw combat power on the battlefield, it revealed a fatal flaw in the concept against an insurgency. Air mobility tactics prevented U.S. forces from clearing and holding an area. Sir Robert Thompson, a veteran of the British effort in Malaya, observed, "you got landed from helicopters and the battle took place, but when the battle was over and you had won the battle, you even went out by helicopter. No one ever walked out."[65] This contrasted with a pedestrian enemy, whose foot mobility and knowledge of the terrain allowed him to dictate when, where, and if he wanted to fight.

After the victory at Ia Drang, MACV realized the 3:1 force ratio it developed earlier was optimistic; the actual force ratio was more balanced due to a seemingly endless supply of VC replacements. This should have compelled Westmoreland to reevaluate his attrition strategy. Instead, he increased the request for additional troops to thirty-five battalions (up from the initial estimate of twenty-four). By the end of 1966, U.S. forces would jump to 385,300 in the hopes of reaching the crossover point.[66]

The war shuffled into 1967 with no sign of progress. U.S. troops killed thousands of enemy soldiers in battle, but there was no sign of breakdown in the enemy's will to fight or his ability to repopulate combat forces. Convinced he was close to the crossover

---

[64] Doughty, *The Evolution of U.S. Army Tactical Doctrine*, 30-32.

[65] W. Scott Thompson and Donaldson D. Frizzell, eds., *The Lessons of Vietnam* (New York: Crane, Russak, 1977), 178.

[66] The crossover point is where the enemy's personnel losses exceed his ability to replace them. Dominic D.P. Johnson, *Overconfidence and War: The Havoc and Glory of Positive Illusions* (Cambridge, MA: Harvard University Press, 2004), 156, http://site.ebrary.com/lib/nationaldefense/ Doc?id=10314232 (accessed March 4, 2012).

point, Westmoreland called for an increase in soldiers to 542,588. Concern over the

Army strategy of attrition manifest within the Pentagon; Secretary of Defense Robert S.

McNamara asked his Systems Analysis Office to calculate the viability of yet another

troop increase. Citing field reports and the Armored Combat Operations in Vietnam

study, the analysis indicated that force increases would have very little impact.[67]

McNamara denied Westmoreland's request, instead agreeing to a cap of 525,000 soldiers.

During this time, the Army chased its elusive adversary through trackless jungles,

catapulting from one fire support base to another in Vietnam. These wild goose chases

culminated in several large force operations at Attleboro (September–October 1966),

Cedar Falls (January 1967), and Junction City (February–April 1967). Leaders deemed

Attleboro a success. Yet despite the loss of 1,100 casualties in the 72-day battle, the VC

reoccupied the area and resumed operations shortly after U.S. forces moved search and

destroy operations elsewhere. Cedar Falls and Junction City confirmed the U.S. belief

initiated at Attleboro: that inflicting high casualties at base camps located away from

population centers kept the enemy on the run, decreased his forces, and enabled other

U.S. forces to implement its pacification program. The enemy saw it differently.

General Vo Nguyen Giap, Commander of the North Vietnamese Army, stated the North's

objective was "draw American forces away from pacification and engage them in

inconclusive battles along the frontiers, inflicting U.S. casualties in the process and

sapping U.S. will to continue the war."[68]

As MACV forces moved away from the coast where the majority of the South

Vietnamese population lived, they failed to provide a shield to protect pacification efforts

---

[67] The reports showed that the enemy initiated 88 percent of all engagements; the enemy had the initiative for when to accept or refuse battle on their terms. Krepinevich, *The Army and Vietnam*, 183, 188.
[68] George C. Herring, *The Pentagon Papers* (New York: McGraw-Hill, 1993), 419, 421.

and turned thousands of residents into refugees as U.S. firepower razed villages across the country. Contrary to the Army belief that it was extending a defensive line against the insurgency, Defense analysts noted "90 percent of all incidents in any given quarter were occurring in the 10 percent of the country that held over 80 percent of the population."[69] In the end, the attrition strategy did not succeed in providing security for the population or a buffer for the RVN to regain legitimacy. After the Tet Offensive provided evidence that two years of search and destroy tactics did nothing to reduce the VC will to fight, MACV shifted the focus of its effort onto pacification under its new commander, General Creighton Abrams.

~ Anchoring and Confirmation Bias ~

As it prepared to transition from an advisory role to a direct engagement role in Vietnam, the U.S. Army anchored on "conventional combat" as exemplified in two World Wars and Korea. The evidence of success was abundant, magnetizing leaders to a style with which they were intimately familiar. Lieutenant General Lionel C. McGarr, the senior leader in Vietnam prior to General Westmoreland, typified this thinking, paying mere lip service to counterinsurgency doctrine. His objectives in Vietnam were to "find, fix, fight, and finish the enemy," the Army's mission in conventional war.[70]

Likewise, Army Chief of Staff General Weaver's assertion that the problems in Vietnam were more military than political or economic reveals his bias towards military action, causing him to frame the present conflict based on past success. As an authority figure, his statements removed any traction counter-guerrilla doctrine had garnered to that point. Army leaders relegated counter-guerrilla warfare doctrine to the 31-series Field

---

[69]Krepinevich, *The Army and Vietnam*, 188.
[70] As chief of the Military Advisor and Assistance Group (MAAG) in Vietnam, McGarr promoted the idea of "search and destroy" operations, referred to at the time as "net and spear" operations. Krepinevich, *The Army and Vietnam*, 57.

Manuals developed by its Special Forces, itself an organizational outlier. Even the Special Forces succumbed to this subtle cognition error, emphasizing the need to fight "fire with fire" in lieu of "pacification" committees in their doctrine. Like other senior leaders, General Westmoreland anchored on conventional warfare but tailored his past-present analogy to Vietnam and Korea. Westmoreland was convinced Hanoi would mass forces to the south similar to action on the Peninsula in 1950, necessitating a large influx of general purpose forces to counter the North's action. Westmoreland's anchor set his paradigm to conventional warfare not only for Phase III of the insurgency in June1965, but well after when the communist insurgency reverted back to Phase II.

The power of confirmation bias is its insidious effect on what information an individual looks for and how he *interprets* it. U.S. leaders skewed the lessons from Greece, Korea, and the Philippines—each of which were applicable in the Vietnam conflict. The Greek civil war validated the idea that general purpose forces, with adequate air support, could prosecute COIN. The Korean War introduced the perception that guerrilla activities precipitated an enemy cross-border offensive with conventional forces. Finally, the Philippines experience advanced the notion that operations should be restricted to securing the population before engaging in limited offensive operations. These conflicts reflected little difference between counterinsurgencies and conventional warfare; leaders did not need to rethink army doctrine "because the results fit so well with the expectations." [71]

Westmoreland fell to the allure of confirmation bias in combat, beginning with the Battle of the Ia Drang Valley, which confirmed the effectiveness of U.S. strategy.

---

[71] Larry E. Cable, *Conflict of Myths* (New York, NY: New York University Press, 1988), 29-33, 63.

Tactically, the strategy of "search and destroy" to force the enemy into a large battle was successful—large battles at Attleboro, Cedar Falls, and Junction City all "confirmed" American instincts. Strategically, Westmoreland's confirmation bias, exhibited by his "more of the same" refrain resulted in failing to reach the crossover point, protecting the population, or buying time for the RVN. His failure to see the conflict as more political than military—despite evidence of the former after Ia Drang—illustrates the power of confirmation bias and its ability to seemingly validate a preconceived notion.

~ Groupthink ~

Applying groupthink to this case is difficult because Westmoreland's role, while primary in Vietnam, was adjunct to President Johnson's closest advisors. As such, the decision-making group includes Westmoreland and Johnson's "Tuesday Lunch Group," illustrating the political-military nexus in the decision to go to war and how to fight it.[72] The first antecedent, "cohesion," is evident in the group. Despite initial objections by Maxwell Taylor, ambassador to Vietnam, all members wanted to escalate involvement to stem Soviet "aggression by proxy." Realizing the U.S. had failed in its advisory role, McNamara pushed Johnson to shift involvement to direct engagement. While the team debated the merits of pacification versus conventional force, Taylor's eventual support

---

[72] The Tuesday Lunch Group included President Lyndon Johnson, National Security Advisor Walt Rostrow, Secretary of Defense Robert McNamara, Secretary of State Dean Rusk, JCS Chairmen General Earle Weaver, CIA Director Richard Helms. David M. Barrett, "Doing 'Tuesday Lunch' at Lyndon Johnson's White House: New Archival Evidence on Vietnam Decisionmaking," *Political Science and Politics* 24, No. 4 (December 1991): 677, http://www.jstor.org/ stable/419403 (accessed March 4, 2011).

for force placed the last brick in the group's cohesive wall.[73] Still, the entire structure almost crumbled under tension among the Joint Chiefs, McNamara, and the President.[74]

A look at the second antecedent, "organizational faults," reveals mixed results. White House documents show that alleged group insularity was untrue. The President sought external advice routinely, which provided the group with a steady stream of cautionary advice about continuing escalation in Vietnam.[75] In contrast, with his close control of the bombing campaign in the north, Johnson abdicated much of his leadership role to MACV for the strategy in the South. Accepting the primary role for planning the war, Westmoreland hewed to the Army totem of large-unit war, despite creative math by his staff to achieve the desired 3:1 force ratio. Finally, McNamara's statement "forces will be used however they can be brought to bear most effectively" reveals the lack of a coherent strategy among the principles.[76]

The stress of potentially losing to communist forces in 1965, and the resultant decision to counter the VC push south, illustrates the third antecedent, "provocative context." Westmoreland's plea to expand involvement, backed by the assessments of McNamara and Taylor, set Johnson on the path of escalation in the North while committing forces in the South. Once there, Johnson continued to support his commander due to the pressure of not wanting to be seen as weak against political

---

[73] Taylor, concurring that a withdrawal would weaken the U.S. image, saw that pacification failed and the Viet Cong was increasing in strength, so the calculus became "how to change a losing game, not call the game off." His approval was a major factor in Johnson's escalation decision. John M. Taylor, *An American Soldier: The Wars of General Maxwell Taylor* (Novato, CA: Presidio Press, Inc, 1989), 321-322.

[74] While the Joint Chiefs were satisfied with the decision to include more troops, they wanted to extend into Laos and Cambodia, which Johnson and McNamara denied, fearing an expanded conflict might involve China and the Soviet Union. Dale R. Herspring, *The Pentagon and the Presidency: Civil-Military Relations from FDR to George W. Bush* (Lawrence, KS: University Press of Kansas, 2005), 171-176.

[75] Barrett, "Doing 'Tuesday Lunch' at Lyndon Johnson's White House," 677.

[76] Krepinevich, *The Army and Vietnam*, 157-159.

attacks, needing congressional support for his "Great Society," and refusing to be the first U.S. President to lose a war.[77]

The first set of symptoms is evident in the "belief in the inherent morality of the group." Politically, all members subscribed to a belief in domino theory, which compelled them to defend South Vietnam at all costs—a loss here would lead to the spread of communism in Indochina. Militarily, this led to committing conventional forces to stop the Viet Cong. After the insurgency reverted back to Phase II, Westmoreland repeatedly asked for more troops to execute his "search and destroy" strategy. Johnson obliged, believing it was a moral obligation to support South Vietnam by "squeezing the enemy" through gradual escalation. Prevented from invading the North to prosecute an annihilation strategy, the army's attrition strategy leveraged U.S. advantages and offered the prospect of a faster victory than a long COIN campaign. [78]

There was evidence of "close-mindedness" in the pursuit of attrition strategy, specifically among Westmoreland and Wheeler. With Johnson focused on the North, Westmoreland was granted *carte blanche* to decide the strategy for the South. While his initial stance was valid based on attacks in 1964, Westmoreland's pursuit of this strategy after VC forces were repelled reflects a closed mind. Trapped in the paradigm of a large-force war, he ignored the failure of ARVN "search and destroy" operations, which "failed to establish any contact with major VC units" and should have compelled him to rethink similar U.S. efforts.[79] Likewise, Wheeler did not recognize that inadequate quick reaction forces were the root cause of ARVN defeat. The fact that U.S. air mobility

---

[77] Johnson, *Overconfidence and War*, 139.
[78] Interview with General Maxwell Taylor, 17 June 1982 quoted in Krepinevich, *The Army and Vietnam*, 165.
[79] Ibid., 167.

provided this capability and enabled a focus on pacification was lost on him. As the campaign plodded along, Westmoreland failed to realize that Attleboro, Cedar Falls, and Junction City did not validate his attrition strategy and that the crossover point was unattainable—two years of executing this strategy failed fundamentally to achieve strategic objectives.[80]

Early in the group's decision to escalate engagement with Vietnam, there was pressure towards uniformity, representing the third set of symptoms. Self-censorship was exhibited by Ambassador Taylor, who finally submitted to Johnson's pressure to "do something" and acquiesced to using large-scale conventional force. There was not an illusion of unanimity in the group, however, as senior officials at the State Department implicitly rejected Westmoreland's assertion that the VC insurgency had reached stage 3, requiring the commitment of forty-four battalions in July 1965. Still, the President's mind was set. He would not deviate from the course established six months earlier.[81]

Similar to the French Army's reliance on methodical battle doctrine in World War II, the U.S. Army's dependence on conventional warfare doctrine, embodied by large unit "search and destroy" missions to execute its attrition strategy, resulted in strategic failure in Vietnam. To varying degrees, leaders in both cases submitted to individual and group biases, cementing their advocacy for a doctrine inappropriate to the combat situation they encountered. The next chapter shifts from a look at cases where an overreliance on established but inappropriate doctrine resulted in failure, to examples where leaders pushed for the use of unproven concepts or technologies, not as mere appendices to established doctrine in war strategy, but as the basis for that strategy.

---

[80] Gary R. Hess, *Vietnam: Explaining America's Lost War* (Malden, MA: Blackwell Publishing, 2009), 90.
[81] Krepinevich, *The Army and Vietnam*, 135.

39

CHAPTER THREE: CASE STUDIES (CONCEPT TO DOGMA)

The next two case studies show the outcome of when a leader blindly champions the use of persuasive, but unproven concepts as the basis of a war strategy. In the third narrative, the U.S. Army Air Force (USAAF) pursuit of unescorted "high altitude precision daylight bombing" theory resulted in combat losses so extensive that bomber units could not generate enough missions to continue executing the air strategy. In the final narrative, U.S. Central Command (CENTCOM) incorporation of "rapid dominance" theory into the Iraq War, under guidance by the Office of the Secretary of Defense (OSD), resulted in an unqualified Phase III success, but resolute failure thereafter.

High Altitude Precision Daylight Bombing: USAAF in World War II

~ Preface ~

The early months of 1943 found the USAAF struggling to gain legitimacy. Within Eighth Air Force (8AF), the VIII Bomber Command faced increased pressure from the Royal Air Force (RAF) to fulfill its role in the Combined Bomber Offensive (CBO) against German industry. Replacing Major General Carl Spaatz as 8AF Commander, Brigadier General Ira C. Eaker echoed sentiments that a daylight bombing campaign against Germany would minimize risk to Allied ground forces for an impending land invasion and possibly negate the need for it. Eaker believed in bomber supremacy and the notion that daylight strategic bombing could be done without fighter escort.[1]

Captain Frank Murphy, a B-17 bomber pilot assigned to the 100th Bomber Group, VIII Bomber Command, also believed in strategic bombing, but was less sanguine about flying deep over enemy territory unescorted. Murphy started flying combat just as Eaker

---

[1] Donald L. Miller, *Masters of the Air: America's Bomber Boys Who Fought the Air War Against Nazi Germany* (New York: Simon & Schuster, 2006), 6.

tasked the vaunted B-17s to strike targets deep into Germany, without fighter escort. Whether due to dogmatic blindness or the lack of technological innovation, no fighter had the range to accompany the bombers all the way to distant targets and back. As a result of this deficiency, Murphy lost many friends to the *Luftwaffe* in the summer of 1943.

Murphy also became a casualty of the USAAF conviction that the bomber will always get through—alone. Flying his twenty-first mission on October 10, 1943, Murphy was piloting his B-17 over Münster, Germany when "German fighters came after the 100th in wave after wave."[2] Without escort, the bombers were easy prey for the *Luftwaffe*. Seconds after the initial attack, German fighters had scattered the bomber group's formation. In seven minutes, they ceased to exist as a fighting unit; a few B-17 bombers, including Murphy's, fought their way to the target and dropped their ordnance. As Murphy flew back to the rally point, German fighters swooped in and raked the B-17 with cannon fire. "Almost as soon as we turned there was an explosion behind me and I was knocked to the floor," Murphy remembered. Looking up, he spotted his co-pilot motioning to bail out of the shredded Flying Fortress. During the descent, Murphy saw the sky filled with black flak bursts, swarms of enemy fighters, tumbling B-17s, and enough parachutes to make it seem like an airborne invasion.[3] German forces captured Murphy soon after landing and sent him to an internment camp, where he spent the next two years as a prisoner of war.

Airpower strategists foresaw the bomber campaign over Europe as a battle of machine against machine with little human contact; yet downed airmen like Frank Murphy met the enemy face to face, on his own soil, before a single American

---

[2] Ibid., 17.
[3] Ibid., 18.

infantryman crossed into Germany. The Thirteenth Wing, of which the Hundredth composed one-third of the force, lost twenty-five of thirty B-17s that day; during the "Black Week" of October 10-14, 1943, the Hundredth lost over 200 men, half of its airmen. The squadron had earned its *nom de guerre*, "The Bloody Hundredth."[4]

By October 1943, VIII Bomber Command was losing thirty percent of its aircrew each month.[5] Morale plummeted as airmen calculated the odds to finish the 25-mission requirement at just seven percent.[6] They could not sustain such loss and amass enough aircraft to employ against German industrial targets. After these losses (and bad weather), VIII Bomber Command suspended its bombing campaign for four months. During the halt to operations, they reviewed bombing doctrine, which rested on the belief that "a well planned and well conducted air bombardment attack, once launched, cannot be stopped."[7] VIII Bomber Command losses in the summer and fall of 1943 proved contrary; unescorted bombers over enemy territory were no match for German fighters. This realization presented U.S. Airmen with a paradigm crisis, requiring a shift away from the unfounded concepts of High Altitude Daylight Precision Bombing (HADPB).

~ Development of HADPB Doctrine ~

HADPB was rooted in the theories advanced by airpower pioneers during the interwar years. Early theorists witnessed the atrocities of trench warfare and saw

---

[4] Ibid.

[5] Spaatz and Eaker calculated a sustainable attrition rate was 5% per month. James Parton, "Air *Force Spoken Here": General Ira Eaker and the Command of the Air* (Bethesda, MD: Alder & Alder, Publishers, Inc., 1986), 172 quoted in Kirk W. Hunsaker, "The Invincible Bomber: Perspectives on the Recognition and Prevention of Airpower Crisis," (master's thesis, Air University, 2005), 22, http://www.dtic.mil/dtic/tr/ fulltext/u2/a477072.pdf (accessed February 11, 2012).

[6] Before May 1944, a combat tour was 25 missions; in June 1944, an 8AF order changed combat tours to 30 missions for lead crews and 35 missions for the all other crews. Tim M. Trautman, "FAQs about Army Air Force Terms in WWII," 398th Bomb Group Memorial Association, http://www.398th.org/ Research/398th FAQ.html#anchor mission (accessed January 14, 2012).

[7] Statement attributed to Kenneth N. Walker, a strategist and co-author of AWPD-1, the blueprint used to conduct the strategic bombing campaign against Nazi Germany. Haywood S. Hansell, *The Strategic Air War against Germany* (Washington, DC: Office of Air Force History, 1986), 10.

potential in the skies above. Guilio Douhet believed "command of the air" would enable a heavily armed "battleplane" to attack enemy centers of gravity; his concept of urban terror bombing targeted the will of a population, hoping to cause governments to sue for peace sooner and minimize the casualties of war.[8] Witnessing the effects of bombing civilians in London during World War I, Sir Hugh Trenchard recognized the potential for airpower to strike an enemy's heartland and shatter his will to fight. He advocated targeting urban infrastructure as the most effective way to affect civilian morale.[9]

Influenced by Trenchard, Brigadier General William "Billy" Mitchell carried the torch of airpower in the United States after World War I. Like Douhet, Mitchell thought command of the air was a prerequisite to offensive operations against an enemy's vital centers. Distinct from Douhet and Trenchard, though, Mitchell proposed attacking military targets first, thwarting an enemy's ability to fight. Once an air force paralyzed an enemy's capacity to wage war, it could attack other vital centers to force the cessation of hostilities.[10] All three airpower pioneers thought success in warfare required an ability to identify and attack the enemy's center of gravity directly; strategic bombardment—and the heavy bomber—was the most effective instrument to accomplish this task.

Mitchell had a profound influence on the Air Corps Tactical School (ACTS), established in 1920. The ACTS faculty, many of them his protégés, held an unshakeable belief in the primacy of strategic bombardment and the heavy bomber. Advances in targeting optics in the 1930s, especially the Norden bombsight, enabled heavy bombers to

---

[8] Giulio Douhet, *The Command of the Air,* (Washington, DC: Office of Air Force History, 1983), 16.

[9] Phillip S. Meilinger, "Trenchard, Slessor, and the RAF doctrine before WWII," In *Paths of Heaven: The Evolution of Air Power Theory*, 43-45.

[10] Mark A. Clodfelter, "Molding Airpower Convictions: Development and Legacy of William Mitchell's Strategic Thought," In *Paths of Heaven: The Evolution of Airpower Theory*, 86.

strike with pinpoint precision.[11] Likewise, the operational envelope of the heavy bomber in the 1930s allowed it to fly beyond the reach of anti-aircraft artillery and fly higher and faster than pursuit fighters.[12] This aura of precision and invincibility allowed the ACTS to propose the adoption of daylight strategic bombing concepts as doctrine.

Tacitly accepting Douhet's vision of a "superbomber," the schoolhouse shunned the need for long-range escorts, viewing the use of fighters as limited to area defense. ACTS texts stipulated, "escort fighters will neither be provided nor requested unless experience proves that bombardment is unable to penetrate such resistance alone."[13] The simplicity of this theory—that a singular type of aircraft could win wars without grievous loss of life—was appealing to a military, a political establishment, and an American public "wary of long wars, but less aware that combat always confounds theory."[14]

A foundational concept taught at the ACTS was industrial web theory, which held that a nation's ability to pursue war depended on maintaining a closely-knit industrial fabric. Precision bombing could destroy this fabric, air planners believed, because their

---

[11] Linking the aircraft's navigation system to the bombardier's optical sight in order to increase bombing accuracy, the Norden bombsight went through significant development in the 1920s for the U.S. Navy before the U.S. Army Air Corps acquired it in 1932. Airmen considered the purported accuracy remarkable at the time, with some bombardiers boasting of dropping bombs into a 100-foot circle from an altitude of 20,000 feet. John T. Correll, "Daylight Precision Bombing," *Air Force Magazine*, October 2008, under "Norden Bombsight," http://www.airforce-magazine.com/MagazineArchive/Documents/2008/October%202008/1008daylight.pdf (accessed April 7, 2012).

[12] In 1935, the B-17's operational ceiling on the was 35,800 feet, while the tactical range of Germany's most widely fielded anti-aircraft gun, the 88mm FlaK-36, was 25,000 feet at seventy degrees elevation. Larry Dwyer, "Boeing B-17 Flying Fortress," The Aviation History Online Museum, http://www.aviation-history.com/ boeing/b17. html (accessed February 26, 2012); Lone Sentry, "Firing Tables – Technical Manual E9-369A: German 88-mm Antiaircraft Gun Materiel," Lone Sentry, http://www.lonesentry.com/ manuals/88mm-antiaircraft-gun/ german-88-mm-firing -tables html (accessed February 26, 2012). Likewise, while German ME-109 and FW-190 fighters were faster than the pursuit planes of the mid 1930s, bomber advocates considered the B-17 immune since it was faster than previous bombers. John Sweetman, *Schweinfurt: Disaster in the Skies* (New York: Ballantine Books, 1971), 30.

[13] Allan R. Millett and Williamson Murray, *Military Innovation in the Interwar Period* (New York, NY: Cambridge University Press, 1996), 124-125.

[14] Miller, *Masters of the Air*, 6.

scientific targeting process identified "those key links in the enemy's economy whose elimination would either cripple his capacity to wage war or...shatter his will to continue fighting."[15]   Likewise, air planners subscribed to the Stanley Baldwin's belief that "the bomber will always get through" and omitted the need for fighter escort into the target area.[16]   Unfortunately for Captain Murphy and the 8AF, the Air War Planning Division's (AWPD) unproven concept of bomber invincibility (which became USAAF doctrine) was proven intellectually and materially deficient in the skies over Germany in 1943.

~ USAAF Strategy over Europe 1942-1943 ~

After the fall of France in 1940, American and British representatives agreed on a combined air offensive against Germany. Based on concepts first debated in the ACTS, the AWPD outlined a six-month offensive against targets that would neutralize Germany and possibly end the war, rendering a land invasion unnecessary.[17] Force planning assumed a ninety percent probability of a bomber hitting its target and included expected attrition due to combat, estimating the need to replace an aircraft every five months.[18]

Escorted by 108 British Spitfires, VIII Bomber Command's first combat sortie was a "milk run" against a railway yard in Rouen, France on August 17, 1942.[19] The next six missions were also within range of British escort fighters against light fighter opposition. These shallow pinpricks provided young bomber crews an opportunity to cut

---

[15] Barry D. Watts, *The Foundations of U.S. Air Doctrine: The Problem of Friction in War* (Maxwell Air Force Base, AL: Air University Press, 1984), 22.

[16] Phillip S. Meilinger, "Giulio Douhet and the Origins of Airpower Theory," in *The Paths of Heaven: The Evolution of Airpower Theory*, 20.

[17] Peter R. Faber, "Interwar U.S. Army Aviation and The Air Corps Tactical School: Incubators of American Airpower," In *The Paths of Heaven: The Evolution of Airpower Theory*, 224.

[18] Pre-war estimates of heavy bomber totals for the air offensive amounted to 11,000 aircraft (770 replacements per month). Hansell, *The Strategic Air War against Germany*, 34.

[19] This was due to competing priorities with other types of aircraft produced stateside as well as the diversion of existing air assets to other theaters, including the Pacific and North Africa. Henry H. Arnold, *Global Mission* (Blue Ridge Summit, PA: TAB Books Inc, 1989), 312; Hansel, *The Strategic Air War against Germany*, 69.

their teeth and work on tactics, albeit under the protection of a large umbrella of fighter

escort. By December 1942, VIII Bomber Command had not fully tested German air

defenses. Despite this lack of validation, Spaatz and Eaker remained confident in the

self-defense qualities of the B-17 and the skill of 8AF airmen.[20] Neither leader saw the

contingent of British escort fighters as a key factor in those early successes over France.

As such, they did not consider the need to procure and field a long-range escort fighter.[21]

By January 1943, the limited success of 8AF bombing stirred a debate as to its

utility at the Casablanca Conference. Citing the large percentage of failed U.S. missions,

the RAF felt it was "carrying the weight" of the offensive. Churchill commented that

"the Americans had not yet succeeded in dropping a single bomb in Germany" and

wanted to integrate 8AF operations into the RAF night bombing campaign.[22] Eaker,

citing adverse weather and limited air assets due to the demands of 15th Air Force in

North Africa, persuaded Churchill to give 8AF more time. Eaker now faced increased

pressure to prove daylight precision bombing in the Combined Bomber Offensive.[23]

The CBO divided targets into four phases based on theater objectives and

projected bomber strength. In Phase One, missions would focus on U-boat facilities

within the range of fighter escort as the Battle of the Atlantic remained delicately poised.

In Phase Two, twenty-five percent of CBO missions would remain focused on submarine

---

[20] Eaker wrote to Arnold in December 1942 stating, "the B-17 has demonstrated…it is the best daylight bomber… it is the only one which completely demonstrated its ability to defend itself from enemy fighters and to fly at an altitude where it does not suffer losses from anti-aircraft fire." Sir Charles Webster & Noble Frankland, *The Strategic Air Offensive Against Germany 1939-1945* (London, England: Her Majesty's Stationary Office, 1961), 451.

[21] Spaatz thought 1,500 bombers and 800 fighters would provide "complete supremacy over Germany within a year." Letter, Spaatz to Arnold, August 24, 1942, Spaatz Papers, MD, LC quoted in Geoffrey Perret, *Winged Victory: the Army Air Force in World War II* (New York: Random House Inc, 1993), 246.

[22] Kent R. Greenfeld, *American Strategy in World War II: A Reconsideration* (Baltimore, MD: Johns Hopkins Press, 1963), 92.

[23] Hansell, *The Strategic Air War against Germany*, 70.

facilities, with the remaining seventy-five percent concentrated on fighter aircraft factories within a 500-mile radius—the Allies needed air supremacy for the upcoming land invasion. In Phase Three, the Allies would commit 1,746 projected bombers to any required tasks. In Phase Four, over 2,700 bombers would be limited only by their combat radius, which at 2,000 miles allowed bombing missions deep into Germany.[24]

On January 27, 1943, VIII Bomber Command B-17s extended beyond the range of their fighter escort. Ninety-one bombers attacked German submarine pens, with fifty-three B-17s dropping their ordnance on target while suffering three combat losses. Convinced the AWPD strategy was showing its success, Eaker directed his airmen to extend the offensive deeper into Germany. Eaker's bombers could not avoid German fighters, let alone outrun them. Without fighter protection, the bombers had to rely on mutually supportive "box formations," which offered marginal defense against the *Luftwaffe*. Combat losses increased sharply by April 1943. The VIII Bomber Command had started their baptism by fire.[25]

June 1943 saw the Germans increasingly prepared for Allied bombing excursions into Germany. The *Luftwaffe* concentrated seventy percent of their fighters along the western border to counter the Allied strikes. Established in five defensive bands twenty-five miles deep, German fighters operated within an integrated network of early warning radars and anti-aircraft flak guns to provide sector defense.[26] The defensive shield over Germany caused the Combined Chiefs of Staff to change CBO targeting priorities. The Pointblank Directive made destruction of the *Luftwaffe* the main CBO objective, targeting

---

[24] David MacIsaac, *Strategic Bombing in World War Two: The Story of the United States Strategic Bombing Survey* (New York, NY: Garland Publishing Co., 1976), 258.

[25] 8AF lost 26 of 122 B-17s over Bremen and 26 of 60 over Kiel, losses of 21 and 43 percent. Noble Frankland, *Bomber Offensive: Devastation of Europe* (New York: Ballantine Books, 1970), 75.

[26] Perret, *Winged Victory*, 249.

aircraft installations and factories.[27] Eaker welcomed the focus onto the B-17's biggest

threat. Elimination of German fighter production coupled with combat losses would

cause the *Luftwaffe* to lose a battle of attrition against an ever-larger bomber force; but

German factories lay deep inside Germany, under the fabric of seasoned air defenses.[28]

Three weeks after a failed attempt to curb German fighter production in July

1943, B-17 crews briefed the largest U.S. bomber attack to date against Regensburg and

Schweinfurt, deep in Bavaria.[29] Set for August 17, 1943, the raid called for 146 bombers

to strike Regensburg first. Minutes after the Regensburg force crossed the North Sea, a

second group of 230 bombers would fly the same route before splitting to attack

Schweinfurt. After a 90-minute takeoff delay due to adverse weather, the Regensburg

force took to the skies; three and half hours after the Regensburg force departed, the

Schweinfurt force lifted off. The gap allowed the Germans to hit the Regensburg

formation then regroup to hit the Schweinfurt formation. VIII Bomber Command lost

147 B-17s on the "double strike" mission—forty percent of its force that day.[30]

While these results convinced Arnold of the failure of unescorted bombing, this

new reality was at odds with how he planned to lead the USAAF into independence. To

Arnold, the future "thousand bomber fleet" was that avenue, but traveling this road

---

[27] Sweetman, *Schweinfurt: Disaster in the Skies*, 128-129. The Pointblank Directive mixed false optimism with reality, stating, the "destruction which is being inflicted by our…bomber force [has] forced the enemy to deploy day and night fighters in increasing numbers…Unless this increase in fighter strength is checked, we may find our bomber forces unable to fulfill the tasks allotted to them. To this end…British and American bombers… shall attack German fighter forces and the industry on which they depend." Martin Middlebrook, *The Schweinfurt-Regensburg Mission* (New York: Charles Scribner's Sons, 1983), 31.

[28] Frankland, *Bomber Offensive*, 53.

[29] Perret, *Winged Victory*, 262-263; Eaker responded to condolences offered by Spaatz, stating, "we will repeat this effort many times and on an ever-increasing scale." Martin W. Bowman, *The Mighty Eighth at War: USAAF 8th Air Force Bombers Versus the Luftwaffe, 1943-1945* (Barnsley, Yorkshire: Pen & Sword Aviation, 2010), 8.

[30] Roger A Freeman, Alan Crouchman, and Vic Maslen, *Mighty Eighth War Diary* (London, England: Jane's, 1981), 89-90.

48

demanded positive results in the present. Arnold urged Eaker to return to Schweinfurt to finish the job as soon as possible.[31]

Mission #115 on October 14, 1943 marked that return trip to Schweinfurt. "Black Thursday" involved the greatest air engagement up to that time—a titanic struggle between two air armadas. Two hundred twenty-nine bombers fought 300 fighters for three hours along a battle line that extended for 800 miles. In the aftermath, only thirty-three of Eaker's bombers landed without damage; 8AF suffered 642 casualties among 2,900 combatants.[32] Eaker knew his deep strikes were finished until a viable long range escort fighter arrived in December 1943 in the form of the P-51 Mustang. This marriage of air capabilities meant the end of German air superiority was near.

~ Anchoring and Confirmation Bias ~

Airmen in the interwar years had no real-world experience on which to anchor. Viewing the Western Front in World War I, they just knew that anchoring on the ground was *not* the solution for the future. A look to the heavens presented a rosier outlook; the shock of German zeppelins over London offered potential for a future "superbomber." To them, the Martin B-10 bomber represented the manifestation of strategic bombing, moving an ethereal concept to tangible possibility with its production in 1932—the anchor was dropped.[33] Strategic bombardment framed everything—theories, doctrine, materiel—for airmen still seeking an identity in a land- and sea-dominated military.

With the paradigm anchored on strategic bombing, Arnold and Air Corps leaders exhibited confirmation bias towards the strategic bomber, securing its status in the air

---

[31] Miller, *Masters of the Air*, 204.
[32] Ibid., 212.
[33] The 1930 Martin B-10 Bomber was an all metal, twin-engine, monoplane with an enclosed cockpit and retractable landing gear capable of a top speed of 200 mph and a bomb load capacity of 2,000 lbs. It was in this plane that Lieutenant Colonel Henry Arnold made his famous non-stop flight from Alaska to Seattle in 1934. Sweetman, *Schweinfurt: Disaster in the Skies*, 15-17.

arm relative to pursuit aircraft. With its introduction in 1935, the B-17 exhibited the range, speed, and payload required to implement the Air Corps' keystone doctrine. Arnold was elated, stating that the B-17 exemplified "airpower you could put your hands on...for the first time in history."[34] Scant debate occurred on improving pursuit aircraft because few believed it was technically possible to develop a fighter that could match the bomber in both range and speed.[35] General Laurence S. Kuter and other bomber advocates mirror-imaged this assumption onto the adversary: if the U.S. could not develop an advanced fighter, neither could the enemy. Similarly, manuals proved the ceiling of the B-17 exceeded the effective range of American, and thus, German anti-aircraft guns, leading airmen to assume the B-17 was indefensible. Both assumptions proved inaccurate.[36]

Spaatz and Eaker exhibited confirmation bias toward unescorted bombing on the first mission into occupied France. The August 17, 1942 raid over Rouen was successful because of the 10:1 ratio of Spitfires to B-17s. Despite this rational explanation for success, their "mind's eye" deceived them into confirming preconceived notions of bomber superiority. As 8AF combat losses increased sharply, the power of Eaker's flawed paradigm was revealed in his dismissal or rationalization of reports that showed

---

[34] Thomas H. Greer, *The Development of Air Doctrine in the Army Air Arm 1917–1941* (1955; repr., Washington, DC: Office of Air Force History, U.S. Air Force, 1985), 47 quoted in Robert A. Eslinger, "The Neglect of Long-Range Escort Development During the Interwar Years" (master's thesis, Air University, 1997), 13, http://www.dtic.mil/dtic/tr/fulltext/u2/a393237.pdf (accessed April 5, 2012).

[35] Eslinger, "The Neglect of Long-Range Escort Development," 14.

[36] Kuter, chief of the bomber section at ACTS, stated he and other bomber advocates closed their minds because of the speed of the B–17. In doing so, they had established a dogma rather than a doctrine for strategic bombing. Ibid., 14. The typical altitude of a bombing mission in 1943 was 25,000 feet, the heart of the envelope for Germany's 88mm and 105mm anti-aircraft guns. Air Force Publication. *Aviation Physiologists Bulletin,* US Army Air Forces, Bulletin No 7., (Sept 1944), 5-6 quoted in James J. Carroll, "Physiological Problems of Bomber Crews in the Eighth Air Force During WWII," (master's thesis, Air University, 1997), 21, http://www.dtic.mil/dtic/tr/fulltext/u2/a398044.pdf (accessed April 5, 2012).

massive bomber losses. The consequence of enduring so many losses strengthened Eaker's resolve regarding the imperative of strategic bombing, albeit in a perverse way.

Recognizing a growing problem with German fighter defenses, the Pointblank Directive tasked 8AF bombers to strike at fighter production facilities instead of waiting for a long-range escort fighter. From Blitz Week in July 1943 to "Black Thursday" in October, Eaker was blinded to the magnitude of losses, irrationally thinking that ever larger formations of bombers were the answer. The shock of losses during Black Week finally awakened Eaker from his stupor, shocking him from his paradigm. Strategic bombing was still of import, but not without fighter escort on the wing. When the clouds finally cleared after a gloomy three months, the P-51 arrived in theater as the long-range fighter escort. The end of German air superiority was near.

~ Groupthink ~

Cohesion was prevalent among USAAF leaders in World War II, illustrating the first antecedent. This cohesion first formed at the court martial of Billy Mitchell in 1925, when airmen like Arnold, Spaatz, and Eaker testified on the poor status of American airpower.[37] As the bombing mission grew, these airmen were promoted to higher grades, permeating centers of power in the Air Corps and shaping policy.[38] All had taught at or were graduates of the ACTS, which by the mid-1930s was teaching "invincible" bomber doctrine.[39] All identified themselves as airmen, a new breed of "air-minded" warriors united in purpose to establish a separate air service under the theory of strategic bombing.

---

[37] Carl H. Builder, *The Icarus Syndrome: The Role of Airpower Theory in the Evolution and Fate of the U.S. Air Force* (New Brunswick, CT: Transaction Publishers, 1994), 54.

[38] The influence of the ACTS was evident in World War II, as the school graduated 261 of the 320 generals serving in the USAAF at the end of the war. Clodfelter, "Molding Airpower Convictions," 83.

[39] After a fierce debate between bomber and fighter factions at the ACTS, the support of two Air Corps chiefs—Generals Oscar Westover and Hap Arnold—tipped the scales in favor of strategic bombing. Hunsaker, "The Invincible Bomber," 57.

Organizational faults were present in the upper strata of the USAAF. Certainly its doctrine, HADPB, was the product of an institution isolated at Maxwell Field, Alabama. By the mid-1930s, sixteen of the seventeen instructors were graduates of ACTS, evidence that "students became instructors and passed down theory as fact."[40] As World War II drew near, the Air Corps enlisted help from this parochial think-tank; as a result, ACTS instructors with a bias towards strategic bombardment dominated the planning process, moving bombing theory into wartime strategy. The group was homogenous, sharing not only a tradecraft, but a vision for a separate service. This drive for autonomy centered on the bomber and its prophesied ability to attack an enemy's center of gravity directly. The path from airpower theory to operational reality was populated with like-minded airmen.

The stresses to showcase the efficacy of strategic airpower were overwhelming. A matter of life and death for bomber crews over Germany was a metaphor for the fate of the USAAF as a separate service. Despite accumulating bomber losses in the summer of 1943 and knowledge that there was no long-range escort fighter, Arnold believed Germany was close to defeat. Pushing Eaker for maximum effort every mission, he diverted fighter aircraft to England to help. Arnold's credibility with the Allies, the President, and the other service chiefs was at stake. Eaker felt the pressure, too. Believing Germany was close to its end, he concluded it was in the best interest of 8AF to continue attacking high priority targets and believed this would potentially end the

---

[40] Sean H. Seyer, "The Plan Put into Practice: USAAF Bombing Doctrine and the Ploesti Campaign," (master's thesis, University of Missouri – St. Louis, 2009), 17, http://auburn.academia.edu/ SeanSeyer/Papers/451576/The_plan_put_into_practice_USAAF_bombing_doctrine_and_the_Ploesti_campaign (accessed December 17, 2011).

war. Eaker thought his resolve would validate airpower theory and lead to a separate

service. To him, the prize of independence outweighed the very real risk of failing. [41]

Given the presence of antecedent conditions, USAAF leadership exhibited both

symptoms of overestimating the group's abilities. All disciples of daylight strategic

bombing held an unquestioned "belief in the group's morality." While they realized the

genesis of airpower arose from the trenches of World War I, they did not subscribe to the

use of airpower as an indiscriminate tool of shock and terror. They preached precision,

and thought daylight strategic bombing was the moral application of airpower—bombing

at night was too indiscriminant. They also suffered from an "illusion of invulnerability."

When HADPB doctrine gained a following in the mid-1930s, pursuit aircraft did not

match bomber performance. This resulted in ACTS cadre thinking pursuit aircraft were

not necessary; senior leaders, forced to make budget decisions in a tough budget climate,

opted to buy bombers instead of pursuit fighters.

The second set of symptoms, close-mindedness, appears in the efforts of the

group to rationalize the vulnerability of the "invincible" bomber in light of real-world

examples in the Spanish Civil War in 1936. Believing the conflict did not represent a

real test of modern airpower, the group questioned the evidence rather than considering

possible fixes. Ultimately, they saw nothing in aerial warfare over Spain to suggest

changing their doctrine.[42] Shortly after the catastrophic losses in October 1943, Eaker

---

[41] Evaluating 8AF losses, Eaker assessed how much attrition was tolerable. The normal acceptable attrition rate was five percent, thus when Assistant Secretary of War Robert A. Lovette suggested a loss of 15% over Schweinfurt equated to three days at 5%, Eager concluded it made sense statistically – especially if destruction of the target might end the war. James Pardon, "*Air Force Spoken Here": General Ira Eaker and the Command of the Air* (Bethesda, MD: Alder & Alder, Publishers, Inc., 1986), 306.

[42] The AWPD, who had witnessed the role of radar and fighter protection in the Battle of Britain as well as the vulnerability of British B-17s against German air defenses, argued that "American bombers were better armed; American formations were tighter" and they would get through. Wesley Frank Craven

rationalized that increased German opposition during Black Week might be the final stand of an enemy struggling under aerial attack. In a letter to Arnold, he commented "this does not represent disaster; it does indicate that the air battle has reached its climax."[43]

Pressure towards uniformity was exhibited by former ACTS instructor Kenneth Walker as the "mind-guard" in the AWPD, "protecting the group from doubts about… their decisions." Walker was "the aggressive advocate who brooked no doubts and drove policy as relentlessly as he drove himself."[44] There was also an "illusion of unanimity" in the group. Eaker and Arnold both understood the importance of long-range escort fighters. Yet Arnold implored Eaker to continue bombing despite tragic losses beginning in June 1943, before replacing him with the popular Jimmy Doolittle. This cast Eaker as a political victim due to his own adherence to the invincible bomber legacy.

The desire to obtain status as a separate service consumed USAAF leaders, to the point where the means of achieving this independence, "strategic bombardment," almost became an end unto itself in 1943. Individual and group cognition biases contributed greatly to this shift, reinforcing misperceptions about the infallibility of advanced technology (in this case, the heavy bomber) despite evidence to the contrary. Yet as the next case study highlights, USAAF leaders were not alone in falling prey to cognitive errors in the challenge of balancing established doctrine with unproven concepts in war.

---

and James Lea Cate, *The Army Air Forces in World War II. Volume 1, Plans and Early Operations, January 1939 to August 1942* (Chicago: The University of Chicago Press, 1948), 600-601.
    [43] Ira C. Eaker, Letter to Arnold, 15 Oct 43, Eaker Papers, Library of Congress, quoted in Hunsaker, "The Invincible Bomber," 48.
    [44] Martha Byrd, *Kenneth N. Walker: Airpower's Untempered Crusader* (Maxwell AFB, AL: Air University Press, 1997), 28.

Rapid Dominance: U.S. Army in The Second Iraq War
~ Preface ~

On April 7, 2003, Colonel Dave Perkins directed his Spartan Brigade, the Second Brigade of the Third Infantry Division (3rd ID), as it blasted into Baghdad, leading the famed "Thunder Run" to Saddam Hussein's Presidential Palace. The fight for Baghdad, while not the protracted siege some had predicted, was far from easy; Perkins' charge marked the "turning point of the war both militarily and psychologically" and brought the conflict to a decisive climax.[45] Two days later, a 3rd ID patrol moved in to investigate noises coming from the Iraqi Ministry of Justice. They were met by young Iraqis stealing computers and tossing thousands of ministry files out windows, blanketing the courtyard below with paper. The patrol radioed for guidance. For months, they had focused on how to defeat the Iraqi military; there was limited discussion of what to do after Baghdad fell. Word came back to the patrol: "secure the perimeter…but don't shoot the looters."[46]

Operation IRAQI FREEDOM (OIF) was a war the United States had rehearsed since the previous campaign ended twelve years earlier. As U.S. and British land forces stormed into Iraq on March 20, 2003, their air forces unleashed a barrage of high-tech firepower on Baghdad.[47] On the ground, coalition forces planned and attacked faster than the enemy, leaving the Iraqi Army confused and defeated. After a decade of buildup, the war lasted less than six weeks, with President Bush hailing the end of major combat operations on May 1, 2003. The new American way of war based on "rapid dominance" concepts had succeeded, cementing its role in post-9/11 military strategy.

---

[45] Mark Bowden, foreward to *Thunder Run: The Armored Strike to Capture Baghdad,* by David Zucchino (New York: Grove Press, 2004), xi.

[46] Zucchino, *Thunder Run*, 318.

[47] The Air Campaign started on March 19, 2003 when two F-117s attempted an unsuccessful decapitation strike at Dora Farms. Williamson Murray and Robert H. Scales, *The Iraq War: A Military History* (Cambridge, MA: Harvard University Press, 2003), 155.

The honeymoon period lasted only a short time as post-Saddam Iraq descended into chaos, calling the Pentagon's bet on a small-force strategy. The margin call found postwar planning insufficient—although "rapid dominance" worked brilliantly in knocking Saddam from power, it led to a wrongly-sized and ill-prepared force to conduct peacekeeping operations. Iraqis revolted, leading to an insurgency. After the bombing of the UN Headquarters in Baghdad on August 19, 2003, U.S. forces played a desperate game of catch up, dusting off decades-old COIN doctrine to address the insurgency. The subsequent eight and a half years took their toll. By the time the last soldier left Iraq on December 17, 2011, the U.S. had suffered 4,422 fatalities and 31,922 wounded.[48]

~ Evolution of Rapid Dominance ~

Secretary Rumsfeld wanted to recast the military into a leaner force to meet the challenges of the 21st century. Based on briefings on the revolution of military affairs (RMA) from the Defense Department's Office of Net Assessment, Rumsfeld spawned a new era of "transformation" in the Pentagon. To him, the biggest obstacles to this agenda were the service chiefs and bureaucracy. This rift with senior officers grew during the run-up to Iraq, during which time Rumsfeld showed "contempt for the accumulated wisdom of the military profession." Channeling the invasive practices of the Johnson administration, he advocated unproven concepts in an attempt to exploit the advances in technology and moderate a military he perceived as too influential within Washington.[49]

"Shock and Awe" was one of those concepts, first coined by Harlan K. Ullman and James P. Wade in a 1996 paper, "Shock and Awe: Achieving Rapid Dominance." In

---

[48] iCasualties.org, "Iraq Coalition Casualty Count," iCasualties.org, http://www.defense.gov/news/casualty.pdf (accessed December 21, 2011).
[49] Michael R. Gordon and Bernard E. Trainor, *Cobra II: The Inside Story of the Invasion and Occupation of Iraq* (New York: Pantheon Books, 2006), 4-8.

the debate over the RMA, the paper was an attempt to move from the esoteric theories prevalent in RMA literature into a formulated doctrine suitable for war in the information age.[50] "Shock and Awe" incorporated almost every RMA theory from Colonel John Boyd to Admiral William Owens, including knowledge dominance, strategic and tactical paralysis, precision targeting, speed of operations, and collateral damage minimization.[51]

Proposing a transition from "attrition and 'force on forces' warfare," the goal was to "achieve 'dominant battlefield awareness' [and] near-perfect knowledge and information of the battlefield." Rapid Dominance aimed to "affect the will, perception, and understanding of the adversary…through imposing a regime of Shock and Awe." It implied "the ability to control the environment and to master all levels of an opponent's activities." The authors conceived that their theory represented the next logical step in developing a doctrine that would first complement, then replace, overwhelming force.[52]

The paper described the advantage of grafting doctrine onto existing technology to produce systems capable of "Shock and Awe." The concept of a leaner force perfectly addressed the prevailing view that the two-war strategy and its in-garrison requirements were strategically and financially untenable. Likewise, the efficiencies of America's technical sectors far outpaced an inefficient military-industrial complex—future procurement would need to leverage the private sector and commercial technology.

---

[50] Harlan K. Ullman and James P. Wade, *Shock and Awe: Achieving Rapid Dominance* (Washington, DC: NDU Press Book, 1996), http://ndupress.ndu.edu (accessed October 12, 2011).
[51] Keith L. Shimko, *The Iraqi Wars and America's Military Revolution* (Cambridge, MA: Cambridge University Press, 2010), 112. Colonel John Boyd was a fighter pilot and Air Force iconoclast famous for his "OODA Loop" model. For more, see Robert Coram, *Boyd: The Fighter Pilot Who Changed the Art of War (Boston, MA: Little, Brown and Co., 2002)*; Admiral William A. Owens was a staunch advocate for "Systems Theory" and "Net-Centric Warfare." For more, see William A. Owens and Edward Offley, *Lifting the Fog of War* (New York: Farrar, Straus, and Giroux, 2000).
[52] Ulman and Wade, *Shock and Awe*, 9-14.

Finally, the time required to deploy overwhelming force to a hostile environment was unrealistic, and time was a major factor in leveraging America's asymmetric advantage.[53]

Rumsfeld was sold, commending "Shock and Awe" to Franks in December 2001 to help with the campaign strategy. The paper provided a rough outline of what Rumsfeld wanted in Iraq: a "rapidly deployable small invasion force that would exploit the American advantages in information, speed, precision, and air power to bring about a rapid collapse of Saddam Hussein's regime with a minimum of casualties and collateral damage."[54] Franks appropriated the term "Shock and Awe," but not the details.[55] Still, the paper set the tone for discourse between Franks and Rumsfeld over strategy in Iraq.

~ U.S. Strategy in Iraq ~

Throughout 2002, Franks and Rumsfeld debated the size of the invasion force, which ranged from a low of 18,000 troops to a high of 275,000 troops.[56] The Secretary challenged the assumptions of Franks' planners at CENTCOM, pressuring the general to reduce the size of his force and shorten the deployment timeline. During this time, the Joint Staff launched an "Operational Availability" study to look at various war scenarios, including Iraq. The results revealed "new bureaucratic realities within the Pentagon" as much as the impact of technology on the battlefield. Ever since the end of the first Iraq War, critics viewed the "Powell doctrine" with disdain due to its stringent requirement to use decisive military force.[57] Perhaps expectedly, the study proved otherwise, showing that new technology and concepts allowed U.S. intervention to be rapid *and* lethal.[58]

---

[53] Ibid., 7, 15.
[54] Shimko, *The Iraqi Wars and America's Military Revolution*, 144.
[55] Gordon and Trainor, *Cobra II*, 36.
[56] Ibid., 88.
[57] The "Powell Doctrine" necessitated the use of overwhelming military force and required a 6-month deployment of forces into the theater. While the Army believed technological advances increased

While Rumsfeld favored a light force to deploy on short notice, CENTCOM preferred decisive force with overwhelming power in line with the Powell doctrine. The final plan represented a compromise of three plans staffed by CENTCOM. While not as small as Rumsfeld wanted, at 170,000 troops it was a considerable reduction from CENTCOM's request.[59] From his review of the Afghanistan War, Rumsfeld concluded simultaneity and speed could substitute for mass to create strategic paralysis.[60] Accordingly, CENTCOM planners interlaced simultaneity and speed, two spools from the RMA thread bin, into the strategy. After eighteen months of planning, the U.S. was ready to fight a withered foe it had beaten handily twelve years earlier.

As for postwar planning, "the key question was left substantially unaddressed: what to do after getting to Baghdad."[61] Planning for stability operations was shoddy, lacked organizational ownership, and reflected little interagency coordination. After being informed by Defense officials from the beginning that the State Department was responsible for postwar planning, Franks learned that CENTCOM would shoulder this responsibility. Quickly, he established Joint Task Force IV; but after months of work, the task force failed to produce a usable blueprint for postwar Iraq. Much of the work was viewed as "very pedestrian" and discarded summarily by CENTCOM operators.[62]

---

the capabilities of its forces, war involving a regime change could not be waged on the cheap. Rumsfeld's inner circle disagreed, characterizing this "legacy thinking" as out of step with post-9/11 realities. Ibid., 53.

[58] Of critical importance, though, is that the Operational Availability did not address the required forces necessary for postwar stability operations, where "speed" was no substitute for "mass." Ibid.

[59] Tommy Franks, *American Soldier* (New York: Regan Books, 2004), 428.

[60] Shimko, *The Iraqi Wars and America's Military Revolution*, 147. Colonel John A. Warden III was an airpower strategist who helped develop the air campaign for Operation DESERT STORM in 1991. His Five Ring Theory was a key philosophy espoused by RMA advocates. For more, see John A. Warden, III, *The Air Campaign: Planning for Combat* (Washington, DC: Pergamon-Brassey's, 1989).

[61] Ricks, *Fiasco*, 78.

[62] General Franks' biography, *American Soldier*, reveals his focus, using 90 pages to discuss Phase III planning, contrasted with just five pages to discuss Phase IV planning.

In January 2003, Rumsfeld passed responsibility for postwar planning to the newly created Office of Reconstruction and Humanitarian Assistance (ORHA). On February 21-22, ORHA held its first meeting, "the only time the interagency really sat down at the operator level with policy presence and discussed in detail the activities each of the pillar teams had planned." The problems were clear: ORHA was organized too late and under-resourced "for the first step of securing all the major urban areas, let alone for providing an interim police function." Although Rumsfeld was made aware of the inadequate staffing at ORHA, he was never convinced of the personnel shortfall.[63]

As troops marshaled south of Iraq, there was still no plan for postwar operations. Lieutenant General Joseph K. Kellogg, Jr., a member on the Joint Staff recalls, "I was there for all the planning…there was no real plan…the thought was, you didn't need it. The assumption was that everything would be fine after the war, that they'd [Iraqis] be happy they got rid of Saddam." Colonel Gregory Gardner, also a member of the Joint Staff and member of the Iraq transition team, offered "politically, we'd made the decision that we'd turn it over to the Iraqi's in June of 2003…so why have a Phase IV plan?"[64]

The air campaign started on March 19, 2003. Dramatic images showed Baghdad under assault, as the panoply of U.S military power was on full display in the opening salvo of "Shock and Awe." A sophisticated array of sensors seemed to lift "the fog of war," collecting and collating information to build a common picture of the battlespace.[65] The next day, the ground campaign stormed into Iraq, with the 3rd ID and First Marine Expeditionary Force (1st MEF) spearheading the advance as follow-on forces protected the rear. Weaknesses in this strategy were revealed in the first battle of the war at

---

[63] Ibid., *109-110*
[64] Ibid., 110.
[65] Gordon and Trainor, *Cobra II*, 5.

Nasiriyah. The drive to Baghdad left a yawning void of open, rather than "occupied" territory, allowing *fedayeen* irregular forces to fill in the vacuum.[66] Following a week of intense, city-block combat, Task Force Tarawa secured the city and opened the supply lines for 1st MEF in its advance on Baghdad.[67]

As 1st MEF fought through Nasiriyah, 3rd ID continued its swing northwest to the Karbala Gap. In less than three weeks, U.S. forces were on the outskirts of Baghdad. The speed of the advance was astonishing, as American units "would pop up closer to Baghdad than the Iraqi defenders had expected."[68] From just outside Baghdad, U.S. armored convoys charged through the city "Thunder Runs," inflicting the final stages of "Shock and Awe" on an embattled foe. Losses absorbed by the Iraqis included 100 vehicles destroyed and as many as 3,000 troops killed. More telling was the unknown number of soldiers that fled, evident by the discarded uniforms and abandoned tanks. On April 14, 2003, the Pentagon declared Phase III was over essentially. The U.S. won the war it wanted to fight—now it was Iraq's turn.

Shortly after the fall of Saddam's statue in Baghdad, looters started pillaging the city. U.S. troops sat idly on their tanks as mobs damaged the nation's basic infrastructure and institutions of government. Yet "with only two U.S. divisions in a city of five million, it is not clear what they could have done even if they were inclined to act."[69] When asked why soldiers were not stopping the looting, Rumsfeld replied, "freedom's

---

[66] Robert M. Citino, *From Blitzkrieg to Desert Storm: the Evolution of Operational Warfare* (Lawrence, KS: University Press of Kansas, 2004), 298.

[67] Neither side was prepared for the ensuing fight: the fedayeen were outsiders who lacked the local knowledge to defend Nasiriyah; U.S. forces did not want to capture it, hoping to pass through the city quickly, secure the bridges and extend their supply lines. 1st MEF had to fight its way through the town, peeling off Task Force Tarawa to help secure it. John Keegan, *The Iraq War* (New York: Alfred A. Knopf, Random House, Inc., 2004), 153-155.

[68] William Terdoslavich, "From Shock and Awe to Aw Shucks," in *Beyond Shock and Awe: Warfare in the 21st Century* (New York: Berkley Caliber, 2006), 30.

[69] Shimko, *The Iraqi Wars and America's Military Revolution*, 175.

untidy, and free people are free to make mistakes and commit crimes and do bad things. They're also free to live their lives and do wonderful things, and that's what's going to happen here."[70] The critical legacy of those first few days was that no one was in control of the country. "American soldiers…appeared stunned and helpless when faced with unarmed civilians laying waste to the city right before their eyes. If the Americans would not ensure order and provide basic security, who would?"[71]

In the summer and fall of 2003, the incomplete strategy for "day after" combat operations by ORHA and subsequent misguided policies by the Coalition Provisional Authority (CPA) turned lethal for U.S. troops, now viewed as "occupiers" against the Defense Department's every prediction.[72] Despite CPA attempts to install an Iraqi-led Governing Council in July 2003, attacks spread across Iraq. These attacks signaled an insurgency brewing within Iraq; "the choice of targets showed the strategic concept of destroying American will by attacking U.S. forces, any government or NGO supporting the United States, and any Iraqis working for or believed to be collaborating with the United States."[73] Defense officials were reluctant to acknowledge the existence of the insurgency, and a war strategy that hinged on rapid dominance seemed to be neither "rapid" nor "dominant" in the harsh reality of post-Phase III operations. The next eight and a half years witnessed a military that had to reshape itself dramatically to learn how to "win the peace" in a counterinsurgency campaign.

---

[70] Donald Rumsfeld, *Known and Unknown: A Memoir* (New York: Sentinel, 2011), 476.

[71] Shimko, *The Iraqi Wars and America's Military Revolution*, 175.

[72] Insurgencies face three challenges: arming, financing, and recruiting. Critics cite the war plan and subsequent policy blunders as "the major reason that the anti-U.S. forces burgeoned despite their narrow appeal." First, insurgents had ample access to unsecured weapons due to the small U.S. occupation force. Second, the U.S. failed to secure the border between Iraq and Syria, allowing exiled and external sources to fund the insurgency. Third, CPA policies of disbanding the Baath party and the Iraqi army resulted in massive numbers of unemployed men fresh for recruiting as insurgents. Ricks, *Fiasco*, 193.

[73] Thomas X. Hammes, *The Sling and the Stone: On War in the 21st Century* (New York: Zenith Press, 2004), 175.

~ Anchoring and Confirmation Bias ~

Before 9/11, the Pentagon was in turmoil over Defense Secretary Rumsfeld's transformation agenda. The ensuing invasion into Afghanistan provided Rumsfeld with a venue to debut his strategy of a smaller, technologically advanced ground force covered by persistent surveillance and precision fires from the air. Success in Afghanistan offered Rumsfeld evidence that the RMA was here, causing him to anchor on transformation. Seeing resistance by Army leaders, Rumsfeld's decision to set this anchor was charged with emotion, exemplified by critics' assertion that a quick victory in Iraq would "break the spine of Army resistance to his transformation goal once and for all."[74]

This anchor framed the Defense Department's approach to Phase IV operations in Iraq. Over the twenty months of preparing for war, this anchor influenced discussions between Rumsfeld and Franks on troop levels from three variations of Iraq war plans and caused Bush administration officials to think Iraqis would "do the work of Phase IV themselves," reducing the need for a large occupation force.[75] Furthermore, the creation of ad hoc decision groups within the Department contributed to anchoring bias by "adding additional spheres of control that perpetuated the coalition's agenda."[76]

Confirmation biases distorted the policy options available based on seemingly objective analysis. Favorable to his preference for a smaller force, Rumsfeld referenced a 2002 Joint Chiefs of Staff "Operational Availability" study to challenge CENTCOM planning assumptions and cull troops from the war plan. Rumsfeld based his rationale on the correlation between Afghanistan and Iraq "opposing forces," observing that both were

---

[74] Gordon and Trainor, *Cobra II*, 53.

[75] Ibid., 141-142, 151-152.

[76] Ferdinand Hafner, "Cognitive Biases and Structural Failures in United States Foreign Policy: Explaining Decision-Making Dissonance in Phase IV Policy and Plans for Iraq" (master's thesis, Naval Postgraduate School, 2007), 51, http://www.dtic.mil/dtic/tr/fulltext/ u2/a475957.pdf (accessed February 22, 2012).

third-rate militaries that offered little resistance. Additionally, his fervent belief in being prepared to deal with uncertainty perverted into rationale for not having to plan for postwar operations at all. Douglas Feith, Undersecretary of Defense for Policy offered, "being ready for whatever proved to be the situation in postwar Iraq. You will not find a single piece of paper…that says, Mr. Secretary or Mr. President, let us tell you what postwar Iraq is going to look like, and here is what we need plans for."[77] Other defense leaders exhibited confirmation bias for the lighter force. Echoing sentiments from Ahmed Chalabi, Wolfowitz predicted that Iraqis would greet U.S. forces as liberators, reducing the need for a large occupation force. Chalabi's inclusion in the inner circle of Feith's office as a source of "alternate intelligence" was consequential to postwar planning. His success in convincing defense leaders that Americans were welcome in Iraq and that he would establish security quickly after regime change led to several flawed assumptions.[78]

The Defense Department viewed everything through the lens of "transformation." Officials routinely discounted information that did not fit the "narrative" or accorded with the anchor of a smaller force. The message senior military officials received from the Bush administration was one of indifference. An unnamed four-star general recalled:

> The people around the president…*knew* that postwar Iraq would be easy. They were making simplistic assumptions and refused to put them to the test…They did it because they already had the answer, and they wouldn't subject their hypothesis to examination. These are educated men, they are smart men. They are not wise men.[79]

---

[77] James M. Fallows, *Blind into Baghdad: America's War in Iraq* (New York: Vintage Books, 2006), 45.

[78] Senior defense leaders, including Secretary Rumsfeld, Undersecretary Wolfowitz, Deputy Undersecretary for Policy Feith, and Chairman of the Defense Policy Agency, Richard Perle, favored Chalabi and the Iraqi National Congress. Seymour M. Hersh, "Selective Intelligence: Donald Rumsfeld has his own special sources. Are they reliable?," *The New Yorker*, 12 May 2003. http://www.newyorker. com/archive/2003/05/12/030512fa_fact (accessed December 11, 2011).

[79] Ricks, *Fiasco*, 99.

~ Groupthink ~

While other studies look at the National Security Council, this thesis evaluates the group of decision makers in the Department of Defense (DOD), focusing on OSD and CENTCOM. This is appropriate as DOD was the lead agency for planning Phase III and Phase IV in Iraq.[80] A look at the group's cohesion reveals mixed results. While the group shared the goal of removing Saddam from power and OSD members had years of experience working together, OSD and CENTCOM held competing visions for the best way to achieve this goal.[81] Rumsfeld wanted to scrap the existing war plan to advance his transformation agenda; whereas Franks did not subscribe to transformation and wanted to use the existing plan as the basis for his campaign. Although group cohesion was weak, the codified Secretary-Combatant Commander relationship potentially renders this issue insignificant. By law, Franks' position would always subordinate Rumsfeld's.

The second antecedent, structural faults, is widely evident. Understaffed and inexperienced, Feith's office was a black hole that remained "isolated," ignored planning advice from CENTCOM, and failed to solicit experts on the Middle East.[82] Likewise, General Franks' leadership was uneven, focusing too much on Phase III and not enough on Phase IV. "Group norms" were hijacked by select senior OSD members who formed an ad hoc coalition outside the group to shape policy for Iraq. Members of this coalition operated in the capacity of their organizational ties to the group, but used their formal leadership positions to collude on *the coalition's* agenda for Phase IV, while ignoring the

---

[80] President Bush delegated decisions to Rumsfeld for Phase III and Phase IV in Iraq by January 2003. Bob Woodward, *State of Denial: Bush at War, Part III* (New York: Simon & Schuster, 2006), 162.
[81] James Mann, *Rise of the Vulcans: The History of Bush's War Cabinet* (New York: Viking Penguin, 2004), 274.
[82] Ricks, *Fiasco*, 73, 76.

65

products of CENTCOM.[83] Finally, Rumsfeld's reference to the operational study conducted by the Joint Staff as validation of a smaller force pit the Joint Staff position against CENTCOM's, representing a breakdown between OSD and CENTCOM.[84]

The third antecedent, "provocative situational context," is evident in the group. The debate over force strength and "red-lining" of deployment plans was a constant stressor at CENTCOM, persuading them to relent to the Secretary's position. Likewise, while neo-conservative confidence within OSD counters Janis' hypothesis over a *lack* of self-esteem, high self-esteem appears to have contributed to groupthink, causing the group to not consider any shortfalls in their deficient planning for Phase IV. CENTCOM planners also seem to have been a victim of success from Afghanistan, focusing on Phase III operations while conceding their position of using a large force in Iraq.

Analysis of whether the group exhibited groupthink conditions reveals a tentative "yes" due to limited cohesion, warranting further assessment for groupthink symptoms. While belief in the morality of the group was prevalent, there is no link between this belief and groupthink. Some group members were neo-conservatives, and while their Manichean view held the United States and democracy as forces for good in the world, these views preceded formulation of the group.[85] Further, an illusion of invulnerability permeated the group, articulated by the assumption that it would take no more than 135 days from start to finish to wrap up combat operations. Likewise, Secretary Rumsfeld's

[83] This coalition included Vice President Richard Cheney, Iraqi National Congress Leader Ahmed Chalabi, Secretary of Defense Donald Rumsfeld, Deputy Secretary of Defense Paul Wolfowitz, Defense Advisory Board Chairman Richard Perle, Undersecretary of Defense for Policy Douglas Feith, Chief of Staff for the Vice President, Lewis "Scooter" Libby, and Office of Special Plans Director William Luti. Hafner, 30-31; *Rise of the Vulcans*, 238-243; Ricks, *Fiasco*, 31, 56-57; Woodward, *State of Denial*, 128.
[84] Gordon and Trainor, *Cobra II*, 53.
[85] Daniel Scheeringa, "Was the Decision to Invade Iraq and the Failure of Occupation Planning a Case of Groupthink," (master's thesis, Virginia Polytechnic Institute, 2010), 52, http://scholar.lib.vt.edu/ theses/ available/etd-07292010-145020/unrestricted/ Scheeringa DJ T-2010.pdf (accessed March 4, 2012).

conviction that the United States "does not do nation building" led to overconfidence despite Phase IV plans that resembled "a wish list of high hopes and no how-to."[86]

More than any other set of symptoms, the group exhibited close-mindedness. OSD members involved in the ad hoc coalition rejected any idea that ran counter to their idealist view of post-war Iraq, rationalizing such ideas (and stereotyping advocates) as unsupportive of the President's agenda. Similarly, a foundational premise was that Iraqis would greet U.S. soldiers as liberators; this assumption was held with such conviction by senior members of the administration that it was simply rationalized as true. The failure to challenge this and other strategic level assumptions leaked into operational level planning, exemplified by Lieutenant General David D. McKiernan's myopic focus on combat operations.[87]

Finally, OSD leaders enforced pressure toward uniformity, exemplified by Wolfowitz's rebuke of General Shinseki in congressional testimony and Rumsfeld's deployment of two OSD personnel to "help" CENTCOM with planning. Separate from the DOD group, the more influential ad hoc coalition that included Rumsfeld based their actions exclusively on loyalty.[88] As Jay Garner prepared for transition operations in Iraq, Rumsfeld injected himself into the process of picking the ORHA team, insisting Garner remove knowledgeable State Department members as they were, according to Powell, "neither sympathetic nor supportive of the President's goal of democracy in Iraq."[89]

---

[86] Woodward, *State of Denial*, 136.

[87] As the Coalition Force Land Component Commander, McKiernan gave responsibility for Phase IV to his deputy, Major General Albert Whitley, and never received a follow-up briefing. James R. Howard, "Preparing for War, Stumbling to Peace," (master's thesis, U.S. Army Command and Staff College, 2004), 26, http://www.dtic.mil/cgi-bin/GetTRDoc?AD=ADA430508 (accessed January 21, 2012).

[88] Woodward, *State of Denial*, 411.

[89] Bob Woodward, *Plan of Attack: The Definitive Account of the Decision to Invade Iraq* (New York: Simon & Schuster, 2004), 284.

CHAPTER FOUR: ANALYSIS

This chapter summarizes analysis from the four case studies, taking a macro look at how individual and group cognitive biases caused leaders to lose objectivity and advocate for inappropriate doctrine or unproven concepts. Much of how a military fights in the present and future depends on martial traditions from the past—this goes to the heart of doctrine. The military profession is sustained through the careful selection and interpretation of past events. This strong linkage between historic and current events is unique to the military and exposes leaders to cognition biases as they look at the past to frame the present. Such analogies may mislead "without taking adequate account of the difference in circumstances. What is valid in one situation may…be quite untenable the next time it seems to occur."[1]

In every case, leaders exhibited anchoring and confirmation bias as they used selective lessons from history to determine the best way to fight their existential threat. Past successes tended to act as "anchors," causing leaders to bias their searches for information to validate preconceived beliefs of how to conduct their war. Confirmed by unknown cognitive biases, these beliefs worked their way into planning staffs, where cohesiveness, insulation, and stress resulted in groupthink to varying degrees, effectively validating the leader's preconception, stripping away objectivity, and etching in stone his advocacy for a doctrine or concept inappropriate for the conflict.[2]

---

[1] Michael Howard, "The Use and Abuse of Military History," The Army Doctrine and Training Bulletin 6, no. 2 (Summer 2003), 18-19, http://www.army.forces.gc.ca/caj/documents/vol_06/iss_2/CAJ_vol6.2_06_e.pdf (accessed February 24, 2012).

[2] Studies show confirmation bias is more frequent in homogenous groups than in individuals. The "like-mindedness" of the group causes members to focus on information confirming the dominant position, thinking other members will look for disparate information. Dieter Frey, Stefan Shulz-Hardt, and Dagmar Stahlberg, "Information Seeking Among Individuals and Groups and Possible Consequences for Decision

Table 1 provides a summary of the findings based on an analysis of each case. In reference to "anchoring" and "confirmation bias," leaders in each case anchored on technology, either in the form of firepower, a new weapon (aircraft), or sensors and information processing. This substantiates the enduring duality of doctrine, illustrating the challenge of maintaining its stability while keeping it fresh and relevant with new technologies and concepts. Each case study also revealed how real-world experiences function as powerful metaphors that validate an individual's preference for a certain doctrine or concept. These cognitive biases were relatively easy to identify, confirming their regularity and contribution to a leader's flawed decision in war planning or strategy development.

Table 1. Summary of Individual Biases and Groupthink

Organization	Doctrine / Concept	Anchor	Confirmation	Groupthink Conditions	Groupthink Symptoms	Groupthink Influence
French Army (1940)	Methodical Battle (D)	Firepower (Technology)	La Malmaison Montdidier	5/7	7/8	Yes
U.S. Army (1965)	Attrition (D)	Firepower (Technology)	World Wars Greece-PI-Korea	6/7	6/8	Unk
U.S. Army Air Force (1943)	HAPDB (C)	Strategic Bomber (Technology)	B-17 Performance Initial Raids in France	7/7	7/8	Yes
U.S. Army (2003)	Rapid Dominance (C)	Transformation (Technology)	Afghanistan Operational Availability	3/7	6/8	No

The applicability of groupthink theory in each case was more complicated, especially considering the different interpretations on groupthink application.[3] Based on the Groupthink Model in Figure 1 (page 10), this table shows the qualitative scores of each case study based on an "additive" interpretation of groupthink applicability.

Making in Business and Politics," in *Understanding Group Behavior: Small Group Processes and Interpersonal Relations, Vol. 2* (Mahwah, NJ: Lawrence Erlbaum Associates, Inc., 1996), 215-218.

[3] "Strict" interpretation holds that groupthink theory applies only when all antecedent conditions are met. The "additive" interpretation assumes groupthink theory becomes more relevant as more antecedent conditions are evident. The "liberal" view contends that groupthink applicability depends on the set of antecedent conditions found in each situation. Marlene Turner and Anthony Pratkanis, "Twenty-five Years of Groupthink Theory and Research: Lessons from the Evaluation of a Theory," *Organizational Behavior and Human Decision Processes* 73 nos.2/3 (February-March 1998): 107-108, http://carmine.se.edu/_cvonbergen/Twenty-Five%20Years%20of%20Groupthink%20Theory%20and%20 Research_Lessons%_20from%20the%20Evaluation%20of%20a%20Theory.pdf (accessed March 7, 2012).

The French Army (1940) scored five out of seven on antecedent conditions, showing a moderate potential for groupthink symptoms to occur. The two antecedent conditions missing were "insulation of the group" and "lack of norms for methodical procedures." They scored seven out of eight on groupthink symptoms; "self-censorship" was the only symptom not evident. The high score for symptoms suggests a high probability of defective decision-making in the French Army due to groupthink. This was indeed the case, as twenty years of anchoring on firepower and a predominantly defensive doctrine reduced critical thinking among French leaders, making it easier to "go along with the group."

Likewise, the U.S. Army (1965) scored six out of seven on antecedent conditions, suggesting a high potential for groupthink symptoms.[4] "Insulation of the group" was the only antecedent missing. The assessment shows evidence of six out of eight symptoms, with "illusion of invulnerability" and "illusion of unanimity" the only missing symptoms. The score suggests a potential for defective decisions due to groupthink. Here, the influence of groupthink is unknown due to lack of data. While President Johnson and Secretary McNamara's consent to provide Westmoreland with more troops suggests that groupthink pathologies exist, it could also signify simple agreement on a poor strategy.

The U.S. Army Air Force (1943) scored seven out of seven on antecedent conditions, virtually assuring the evidence of groupthink symptoms. A score of seven out of eight symptoms reveals this was true, suggesting groupthink contributed to the decision to engage in unescorted strategic bombing. While groupthink did contribute to the initial implementation of this theory, the important next question is "did groupthink

---

[4] This thesis assessed President Johnson's "Tuesday Lunch Group" and General Westmoreland for groupthink pathologies, of which the U.S. Army was the beneficiary of their decision.

contribute to the dogmatic pursuit of this theory in the face of monumental losses?" The answer is a qualified yes. Despite Arnold and Eaker both knowing that the lack of long-range escort was the reason for bomber losses, they persisted with the campaign hoping to overwhelm the *Luftwaffe*. The pressure to maintain solidarity and unity in those dark days was tremendous. Dissent would have amounted to admitting the doctrine was flawed fundamentally, which carried extreme wartime concerns as well as undermining the *raison d'etre* for the creation of an independent Air Force after the war.

Finally, the U.S. Army (2003) scored three out of seven on antecedent conditions, representing a low probability for groupthink symptoms. Among the missing conditions, the lack of group cohesion and its relevance to the theory's central premise, group consensus, almost ensures groupthink will not occur, regardless of the number of symptoms. Interestingly, the group scored six out of eight on symptoms; only "self-censorship" and an "illusion of unanimity" were missing. The high score on symptoms is coincidental and does not explain why the U.S. went to war based on an unproven theory. "Anchoring" and "confirmation bias" by a strong-willed principle actor, Secretary Rumsfeld, and his top-level support from the Vice President provides a potential answer.

As the case studies show, not all poor decisions are the product of groupthink. The theory merely suggests that the existence of symptoms increases the potential for a poor decision. Groupthink is just one factor that can lead to a poor decision. Other factors include individual and group competency, the impact of heuristics and biases, a lack of information to make a decision, and external / environmental factors. The qualitative analysis of these case studies illustrates the difficulty in differentiating between groupthink as the cause of poor decisions and simple poor decision-making.

CHAPTER FIVE: RECOMMENDATIONS

The complexities inherent in the strategic environment render the navigation of its turbulent waters extremely challenging for today's service professional and the military writ large. As each case study illustrates, even the most seasoned leaders succumb to individual and group biases, constricting critical thinking and injecting error into the decision-making process. Consistently, poor decisions were the result of when leaders oversimplified complex situations into "mental sound bites."[1] On this thread of reductionism, it would be fallacious to recommend simplistic, paint-by-number solutions to assure success; still, some general guidelines can help.

In every case study, a leader's dogmatic advocacy of a doctrine or idea was symptomatic of a larger problem: inflexibility in the organization, the leader, and even the doctrine itself. Thus, select recommendations focus on increasing adaptability in all three areas. Organizationally, this involves institutionalizing a culture of learning and adaptability to operate in an environment marked with volatility, uncertainty, complexity, and ambiguity.[2] Individually, this includes learning to identify and avoid the seductive pitfalls of reductive thinking while developing the conceptual capacity to make sound decisions despite uncertainty. Doctrinally, this involves augmenting the linear constructs in current planning doctrine with collaborative "reflection-in-action" methods to produce broader, more effective operational solutions.[3]

---

[1] Shore, *Blunder*, 221.

[2] Military senior service colleges currently use the term "VUCA" to describe the complexity of the strategic environment. Judith Steihm, *The U.S. Army War College: Military Education and Democracy* (Philadelphia, PA: Temple University Press, 2002).

[3] Blair S. Williams, "Heuristics and Biases in Military Decision Making," *Military Review* 90, no. 5 (September-October 2010): 40, http://www.au.af.mil/au/awc/awcgate/milreview/williams_bias_mil_d-m.pdf (accessed February 26, 2012).

Recommendations for Organizations

~ Learn to Adapt ~

As a technocratic bureaucracy, the military cherishes routines and habits. Rules, norms, culture, and tendencies all contribute as buffers to change and tend to mute its effects.[4] Adaptation tends to be short-lived and "usually falls within the prescribed norms favored by the organization as a whole."[5] While this resistance to change represents the historic paradigm for the military, the contemporary security environment requires a new reality where regular adaptation is the norm. The military's capacity to adapt to this changing environment and counter adaptive adversaries will be fundamental to achieving organizational success as it executes the nation's post-9/11 military strategy.[6]

The U.S. Army showed a unique ability to adapt in post-Saddam Iraq, effecting extensive institutional changes to shift from its predilection for conventional combat to the exigencies of a widespread insurgency. To ensure that a similar degree of adaptation need not reoccur, all service branches need to incorporate lessons from Iraq into their ongoing transformation programs, despite quixotic and comfortable efforts to rebalance and modernize their forces to counter a familiar large-scale conventional threat.[7]

The rebalancing effort should capture and institutionalize the adaptive skills developed over the course of the eight and half years of post-Phase III operations in Iraq, including adaptive decentralization, learning, experimentation, innovation, and

---

[4] Christopher R. Paparone, "The Reflective Military Practitioner: How Military Professionals Think in Action," *Military Review* 88 no. 2 (March-April 2008), http://www.au.af.mil/au/awc/awcgate/milreview/ paparone_mar08.pdf (accessed February 26, 2012); Chad C. Serena, *A Revolution in Military Adaptation: The U.S. Army in the Iraq War* (Washington, DC: Georgetown University Press, 2011), 6.

[5] Serena, *A Revolution in Military Adaptation*, 6-7.

[6] U.S. Joint Forces Command, *The Joint Operating Environment (JOE) 2010* (Suffolk, VA: U.S. Joint Forces Command, February 17 2010), 7-8.

[7] Ibid., 80.

information sharing. Additionally, service plans and exercise directorates should align unit pre-deployment training cycles to maximize training opportunities and prevent "on-the-fly" adaptation among disparate units in theater. Even more importantly, the military should expand its emphasis on interagency training and exercises at the operational level to expose combat units to the nuances of working with other governmental agencies. Finally, the military must avoid "anchoring" on its OIF experience as the boilerplate for success in the international security environment of the future. [8]

The enduring reality is that all militaries "get the next war wrong to some extent."[9] Thus, the true test of the effectiveness of a military organization is its ability to diagnose the situation it actually confronts and then quickly adapt. "The ability to adapt to the reality of war, its political framework, and its technical and industrial modes, and to the fact that the enemy also consists of adaptive human beings, has been the key to military effectiveness in the past and will continue to be so in the future."[10] Imagination and mental agility to envision the future, prepare for it, and then to adapt to surprises will remain the primary determinants of future success.

~ Fight Groupthink ~

Groupthink represents the antithesis of adaptability. Planning cells and senior staffs have the inclination to become homogenous, exposing members to high levels of cohesion and other antecedent conditions of groupthink. Further, it is difficult for a

---

[8] Ibid., 2-5, 153.

[9] Allan R. Millett and Williamson Murray, eds., foreward to *Military Effectiveness: Volume 2, The Interwar Years* (New York: Cambridge University Press, 2010), xv.

[10] U.S. Joint Forces Command, *The Joint Operating Environment (JOE) 2010* (Suffolk, VA: U.S. Joint Forces Command, February 17 2010), 5. The German experience in 1939-1940 illustrates military effectiveness regarding the evolution of operational concepts. Despite a massive victory over Poland, the German Army's high command was dissatisfied with the performance of its combat units, causing them to evaluate the army's strengths and weaknesses and develop a training program to address its shortfalls. The victory over France in May-June 1940 was predominantly due to this introspection. Millett and Murray, *Military Effectiveness*, 13.

group to recognize when it is in the throes of groupthink, highlighting the importance of taking preventative action. Solutions to counter groupthink center on empowering the group to evaluate alternative perspectives throughout the decision making process. One recommendation is to limit premature agreement by forcing heterogeneity in the composition of the staff. If this is not possible and the staff is still overly homogenous, leaders need to establish a devil's advocate or "red team" to challenge the dominant position and force the group to exercise critical thinking skills. The French general staff in the interwar years, dominated by like-minded veterans of World War I who pursued a singular vision of future war, illustrates the necessity of soliciting opposing viewpoints.

Likewise, implementation of an organizational policy preventing staffs from making "final decisions" in initial meetings would prevent "snap decisions." A "second chance" meeting would provide members time and distance from their initial impulses and guard against implementing "quick fix" methodologies.[11] Additionally, tasking several smaller groups to find solutions to the same problem, then combining the groups to analyze and work through the problem together mitigates the possibility of single individuals dominating the entire group.[12] Finally, all of these suggested preventative measures would be more effective with a mere awareness of this stifling group dynamic.

~ Master Metacognition ~

Metacognition is "thinking about thinking," purposely regulating and rearranging the process of thinking to deal with complex problems that require creative and novel solutions. Metacognition helps organize and control a person's thoughts, in the process highlighting personal inclinations for mental traps and cognitive biases. Cognitive biases

---

[11] Linda Henman, "How to Avoid the Hidden Traps of Decision Making," The Henman Performance Group, http://www.henmanperformancegroup.com. (accessed February 21, 2012).
[12] Frey, Schulz-Hardt, and Stahlberg, "Information Seeking Among Individuals and Groups," 226.

can lure otherwise brilliant people into false beliefs and imprudent judgment. They

come under many guises, and avoiding one bias in a certain situation does not guarantee

immunity for the next situation. The two biases discussed in this thesis are particularly

applicable due to the nexus between military doctrine and strategy. The magnetic pull of

history acts as a powerful anchor. Likewise, confirmation bias seduces individuals into

thinking their opinions are the result of objective analysis, when in fact they are not. This

is especially significant within a group, not only because rationality matters, but because

autonomy of thought matters.[13] Knowledge concerning cognition and heuristics can help

avoid reductionist thinking and error-prone group processes, including groupthink.

The military should formalize training on cognition, heuristics, and biases in

military decision-making, adding courseware into its professional military education

curricula, particularly in the leadership modules of intermediate and senior service

colleges. These institutions should develop lessons that highlight the tendency to use

heuristics to simplify and understand complexity, in the process exposing them to

cognition bias.[14] Lessons should teach common cognition biases, draw themes from

historical examples, and emphasize the ease of committing mental errors in the linear

decision-making processes that dominate military planning. To this end, professional

military education should augment its instructional methods from one focused on

teaching the "school solution" to one that leverages shared experiences, creating

opportunities for active experimentation, trial and error, and flexibility of thought.[15]

---

[13] Ibid., 222-224.

[14] Williams, "Heuristics and Biases in Military Decision Making," 41.

[15] Some writers contend that military education simplifies complex systems by focusing on a scientific view and enshrining assimilative knowledge as "objective certainty." Assimilative knowledge, one of four types of knowledge in experiential learning, is codified in doctrine, rules, and "lessons learned," which then modifies the roles, norms, and values of an organization. Over time, best practices become bureaucratized, leading to institutional inertia and a resistance to change. Other knowledge "types" are

Recommendations for Leaders

~ Understand the Role of History ~

Leaders should study history in breadth, depth, and context.[16] Studying in breadth involves observing history over a long epoch of time, searching for trends of change and constancy. Studying in depth involves going "behind the order…imposed by the historian" to scrutinize the skill, planning, courage, and luck involved, understanding that "what really happened" is the "past" and that "history" is merely a historian's interpretation of "what happened."[17] Studying in context reminds a leader that wars are not merely tactical exercises, but rather conflicts between societies. This allows a full appreciation of the conflict by understanding the nature of the societies fighting them, in essence, developing empathy.[18] Studying history in this methodical manner prevents succumbing to the trap of "overgeneralization" inherent in the application of history.

A selective view of the past sets conditions for failure in the present if a leader takes historical events out of context and applies them in generic fashion: history responds favorably to the beatitude, "seek and ye shall find."[19] The misapplication of history is perhaps no more common than in its association with doctrinal principles first

---

divergent knowledge, gained from reflective observation of experiences by group members from a variety of occupations; accommodative knowledge, developed from shared group experiences and active experimentation that entertains new beliefs on a broader scale; and convergent knowledge, in which group members collectively "make sense" of the world and pass this knowledge to others. Christopher R. Paparone, "The Reflective Military Practitioner: How Military Professionals Think in Action," *Military Review* 88 no. 2 (March-April 2008), 68-70, http://www.au.af.mil/au/awc/awcgate/milreview/paparone mar08.pdf (accessed February 26, 2012); Williams, "Heuristics and Biases in Military Decision Making," 41. For more on experiential learning theory, see David A. Kolb, *Experiential Learning: Experience as the Source of Learning and Development* (Englewood Cliffs, NJ: Prentice-Hall, 1984).

[16] Michael Howard, "The Use and Abuse of Military History," 22.

[17] Antulio J. Echevarria II, "The Trouble with History," *Parameters: U.S. Army War College Quarterly* 35, no.2 (2005): 79, http://www.carlisle.army mil/usawc/ parameters/Articles/05summer/ echevarr.pdf (accessed February 13, 2012).

[18] Shore contends that logic based on empathy for an enemy's perspective, or understanding how he thinks, is not a mere act of political correctness, but essential to national security. Shore, *Blunder*, 222.

[19] Jay Luvaas, "Military History: Is It Still Practicable?," *Parameters: U.S. Army War College Quarterly* 12, no. 1 (1982): 85.

espoused by Jomini. The French theorist and his disciples analyzed campaigns throughout antiquity and surmised that success rested on the level of adherence to certain "principles of war," thus codifying the initial link between military history and doctrine.

Clausewitz reminds practitioners that principles are not necessarily backed by historical proof, warning "there are occasions where nothing will be proved by a dozen examples…if anyone lists a dozen defeats in which the losing side attacked with divided columns, I can list a dozen victories in which that very tactic was employed."[20] The wise leader realizes that while history is important to his development, recognition of its frail structure "is the first essential step toward *understanding*, which is far more important in putting history to work than blind faith in the validity of isolated facts."[21]

~ Embrace Uncertainty ~

The natural tendency for humans is to embrace order and avoid chaos, to seek equilibrium and "have the answer."[22] In this context, "order" equates to "predictability" of an expected outcome in a given situation. Here, leaders must guard against developing simple "cause and effect" relationships, noting the difference between causation and correlation.[23] Throughout the decision-making process, leaders need to challenge their assumptions and those of others; failure to do so may prevent the true cause of an event

---

[20] Carl von Clausewitz, *On War*, trans. and ed. Michael Howard and Peter Paret (Princeton, NJ: Princeton University Press, 1976), 200, 202.

[21] There are three dangers to weaving doctrine so tightly with history. First, history can only illustrate something preconceived as true – it cannot actually prove it. Second, doctrine has a natural tendency to judge historical events. Third, a misplaced faith in doctrine can distort history, causing many of its lessons to go unheeded. Luvaas, "Military History: Is It Still Practicable?," 86-88.

[22] Equilibrium forms the theoretical basis for the concept of "the tipping point." This occurs when people move far from equilibrium and approach chaos, the condition where a single small fluctuation can lead to a point of departure into new, uncharted territory. For more, see Malcolm Gladwell, *The Tipping Point: How Little Things Can Make a Big Difference* (Boston, MA: Little, Brown, and Co., 2002).

[23] Mel Schwartz, "Order Out of Chaos—Learning to Embrace Uncertainty," Psychology Today, http://www.psychologytoday.com/blog/shift-mind/200811/order-out-chaos-learning-embrace-uncertainty-part-1 (accessed February 26, 2012).

from being identified. This highlights, once again, the premise that lessons from historical events are not interchangeable—each battle or outcome is unique.

Chaos suggests the opposite of predictability. It is "unknown" territory, far from the state of equilibrium and an individual's comfort zone. Despite its challenges, learning to navigate within this uncertainty and chaos can facilitate vital new learning and foster mental flexibility within leaders.[24] Mental flexibility is important for confronting the dynamic strategic environment, where embracing uncertainty rather than insisting on absolute knowledge can prevent "analysis paralysis." General Lafontaine's reluctance to mount a counteroffensive at Sedan due to an uncertain picture of the battlefield offers an example of the consequences of waiting for perfect "situational awareness."

A leader's ability to embrace uncertainty allows his mental capacity to expand, evolve, and break old paradigms. This does not imply that leaders should stop looking for answers or new ways to solve problems in the fog of battle; it is simply a reminder that explanations are often based on insufficient understanding.[25] The ethos of embracing uncertainty has implications across the military: its acceptance as the dominant condition of war dictates the type of force its leaders design, the training that force conducts, the education of its officers, and the military culture it institutionalizes.[26]

~ Catch a Kingfisher[27] ~

This relationship between instinct and thought highlights the need for leaders to embrace "adaptive change" as they confront the strategic environment. Adaptive change

---

[24] Ibid.

[25] Shore, *Blunder*, 231.

[26] H.R. McMaster, "Crack in the Foundation," (master's thesis, U.S. Army War College, 2003), 15, http://www.csl.army.mil/usacsl/Publications/S03-03.pdf (accessed February 12, 2012).

[27] Subsection adopted from the dictum, "Nine-tenths of tactics are certain and taught in the books; but, the irrational tenth is like the kingfisher flashing across the pool...success can only be ensured by instinct sharpened by thought." T.E. Lawrence, *Seven Pillars of Wisdom: A Triumph* (1935; repr., New York: First Anchor Books, 1991), 193.

does not occur autonomously; it involves the methodical development of conceptual capacity and expansion of a leader's frames of reference. Leaders with highly refined conceptual capacities are intelligent, intuitive, open-minded, flexible, and emotionally stable— important traits for problem-solving in an environment characterized by volatility, uncertainty, complexity, and ambiguity. These personality traits are products of "nurture" more than "nature" and are the results of targeted mental development.[28]

Similarly, leaders should gain an awareness of the different models depicting frames of reference to facilitate "understanding the problem." A leader's frame of reference (the way he observes, interprets, and behaves in the world) provides the foundation for decision and action in a situation. A singular frame of reference exposes a leader to potential cognitive biases, impairing the ability to negotiate the environment. While this is less significant at lower echelons of an organization, it is hazardous as a leader advances through the institution.[29] To counter cognitive biases as well as gaps in knowledge, experience, and ability to process vast information, leaders should expand their frames of reference. Even with an awareness of different ways to frame a problem, leaders need to guard against the tendency to use one preferred frame of reference when another frame would be more appropriate. Complex problems necessitate obtaining more points of view and employing more frames of reference to understand the problem.[30]

---

[28] National Defense University, "Strategic Leadership and Decision Making – Strategic Thinking," http://www.au.af.mil/au/awc/awcgate/ ndu/strat-ldr-dm/pt2ch9.html (accessed March 3, 2012).

[29] Stratified Systems Theory holds that conceptual skills are proportionately more important to leader effectiveness at upper organizational levels, while technical skills are more important at lower levels of organizational leadership. Stephen J. Zaccaro, *Models and Theories of Executive Leadership: A Conceptual/Empirical Review and Integration* (Alexandria, VA: U.S. Army Research Institute for the Behavioral and Social Sciences, 1996), 49-50. For more on Stratified Systems Theory, see Eliot Jaques, "The Development of Intellectual Capability: A Discussion of Stratified Systems Theory," *The Journal of Applied Behavioral Science* 22 (October 1986): 361-383.

[30] National Defense University, "Strategic Leadership and Decision Making – Framing Perspectives," http://www.au.af.mil/au/awc/awcgate/ndu/strat-ldr-dm/pt1ch5 html (accessed March 3, 2012).

Recommendations for Doctrine

~ Maintain "First Among Equals" Status ~

Military organizations must maintain the primacy of established doctrine as the basis for decision making. All four examples highlight the importance of knowing and understanding the tenets and assumptions of doctrine. While doctrine serves as a guide to action, it is critical that military units know their doctrine, its assumptions, and the foundational principles upon which the doctrine rests before they deviate from it. As no two conflicts are exactly alike, doctrine ideally provides a bounded range of solutions to integrate into a strategy; still, organizations and leaders need to be "doctrinally sound, not doctrinally bound."[31] Moreover, if doctrine is inflexible, is incompatible with other doctrine, or does not change rapidly enough to be relevant to the current environment, it can stifle the organizational adaptability of the units that employ it. Even though doctrine is meant to act as a guide for action, when enforced by regulations, overly structured training, and hierarchically supervised professional military education, doctrine becomes "doctrinaire and a barrier to change."[32]

~ Reorient from Simplifying Complexity ~

A continuously changing operational environment demands rapid analysis and decisions in situations where current doctrinal decision-making processes are ill-suited. The Joint Operation Planning Process (JOPP) outlined in joint doctrine is the sanctioned analytical approach for solving problems and making decisions. Combining elements of the U.S. Army's deterministic Military Decision Making Process (MDMP) with its more

---

[31] Attributed to General Richard Neal, USMC. Bruce J. Miller, interview by author, Norfolk, VA, February 15, 2012.
[32] Serena, *A Revolution in Military Adaptation*, 65; Paparone, "The Reflective Military Practitioner, 69.

creative "Design" process, the JOPP essentially "muddies the water" by injecting nonlinearity into a linear process. As in MDMP, the 7-step template outlined in JOPP generates a specific course of action based on assumptions of "technical rationality."[33]

This requires a shift from exclusive use of linear decision-making processes by the joint community and service components to a process that includes improvisation and reflection-in-action theory.[34] Military planning doctrine should become more flexible, reorienting from its current overreliance on accepted techniques stamped with "the authority of science" to one that embraces collaborative inquiry and collective judgment.[35] This doctrinal reorientation would codify earlier exhortations to treat each situation as unique, guard against forming overgeneralizations based on "lessons learned," and constantly challenge the underlying assumptions of the environment, the doctrine, and the strategy.

~ Plan to "Get it Wrong" ~

As the military anticipates the future of war and develops its doctrine to organize, equip, and train its forces, it must remember that all militaries miscalculate the character of war to varying degrees.[36] General Edward S. Meyer, former Army Chief of Staff, warned that military leaders "focus too much on the... greatest scenario and not maintaining sufficient flexibility...to react elsewhere."[37] The important takeaway is that

---

[33] Technical rationality is the "view that we can reduce the elements of a complex system, analyze them individually, and then reconstruct them into a holistic appreciation of the system." Williams, "Heuristics and Biases in Military Decision Making," 51.

[34] These concepts challenge the operations research belief used in military planning that "optimally efficient solutions can be found in inherently social problems." For more, see Herbert A. Simon, *Administrative Behavior*, 4th Ed. (New York: Simon and Schuster, 1997) and Charles E. Lindblom, "The Science of "Muddling Through," *Public Administration Review* 19 (Spring 1959): 79-88, http://www.archonfung.net/docs/temp/ LindblomMuddlingThrough1959.pdf (accessed April 16, 2012).

[35] Paparone, "The Reflective Military Practitioner," 70.

[36] Millett and Murray, foreward to *Military Effectiveness*, xv.

[37] Brian McAllister Linn, *The Echo of Battle: The Army's Way of War* (Cambridge, MA: Harvard University Press, 2007), 207.

doctrine remain flexible.[38] Military leaders will likely not call the future exactly right, but they must think through the nature of continuity and change in strategic trends to discern the military implications in order to avoid being completely wrong.

Doctrine reflects the biases of its leaders, organizations, and the strategy process. Armed with the insight that biases play a large role in doctrinal development, strategists and practitioners who draft doctrine should strive to account for and reduce these biases, maintaining objectivity. Those who use doctrine, to fight or to teach others to fight, should find reason to think critically about each situation rather than accept doctrinal solutions. Acclaimed theorist Michael Howard sums up the necessity of adaptability to the military as reflected in its organizations, its leaders, and its doctrine, suggesting:

> I am tempted to declare that whatever doctrine the Armed Forces are working on, they have got it wrong. I am also tempted to declare that it does not matter that they have got it wrong. What does matter is their capacity to get it right quickly when the moment arrives. It is the task of military science in an age of peace to prevent the doctrine being too badly wrong.[39]

Military effectiveness in the emerging security environment will depend largely on an ability to identify flaws in its vision of the future and adapt quickly, rather than force a preconceived notion to comport with reality.[40] Increasing adaptability in the leader, the organization, and doctrine is the precursor to success in this strategic environment. History has judged harshly those who adopted rigid mindsets and cleaved to the rock of familiarity, and smiled on those who embraced change and adaptability.

---

[38] Army doctrine evolved from rigid "Active Defense" of Europe based on the 1973 Arab-Israeli conflict to the more flexible and innovative "Airland Battle," which incorporated elements of both attrition and maneuver warfare into its concept of the deep battle. For more, see John L. Romjue, *From Active Defense to AirLand Battle: The Development of Army Doctrine 1973-1982* (Fort Monroe, VA: United States Army Training and Doctrine Command, 1984).

[39] Michael Howard, "Military Science in the Age of Peace," *RUSI Journal*, Vol. 119, (March 1974): 4.

[40] Millett and Murray, *Military Effectiveness*, xv.

CONCLUSION

"Guarding against the next great idea" is about being aware of and avoiding cognitive traps, as an individual and an organization. The four cases presented in this thesis provide cogent examples of how individual and group cognition errors contributed to a leader's advocacy for a doctrine or concept that was inappropriate and ill-suited for the conflict in which they were about to engage.

In each case study, the misguided march to ruin started with a myopic reading of lessons from a battle fought at another time to frame a problem in the present. Leaders "anchored" onto preconceptions of what "should" work in the situation facing them, using salient historical events to "confirm" their preconceived idea of battlefield success. "Anchoring" and "confirmation bias" mixed to develop an innovation-stifling environment that limited the leader's perspective, narrowed his frame of reference, and confiscated his objectivity in a group setting. Surrounded by like-minded individuals solidified his preconceived notion, often to the point where advocacy of a position turned into dogma. Although groupthink was not a contributory factor in every case study, leaders should still be aware of its potential to infect decision making and take proactive measures to prevent it.

The thesis highlighted two distinct paths that leaders followed in the diversion from sound and appropriate doctrine. Along the first path, leaders dogmatically advocated for the use of inappropriate doctrine in their war strategy. The first stop along this path, the widely documented failure of the French Army in the interwar years culminating with the Battle of France in 1940, highlights the danger of basing an entire military apparatus— organizing, training, equipping a force—from just two "best of" examples in combat. General Gamelin's resounding failure in 1940 was the product of a series of missteps over the previous twenty years prior to those decisive points on the Belgian plains. The next stop discussed General Westmoreland's dogged pursuit of a "search and destroy" campaign in Vietnam based on attrition warfare. Here, he shunned counterinsurgency doctrine, deferring instead to a tradition of conventional firepower and tactics. The strategic realities of a "worst case" war with the Soviet Union had shaped the force structure and strategy to which Westmoreland had grown so accustomed, leaving him ill-prepared to fight a more appropriate counterinsurgency campaign.

Departing this path takes the reader to the other, where leaders advocated for unproven concepts in lieu of established doctrine. First, the U.S. Army Air Force experienced heavy losses pursuing daylight strategic bombing over Germany in 1943. Despite escalating evidence that the highly-touted theory of unescorted "high altitude precision daylight bombing" was flawed fundamentally, General Eaker continued to push VIII Bomber Command to the brink of mission failure. Not until they were unable to generate combat sorties in the numbers demanded by Eaker did he grasp the cold realities of life over the skies of Germany and change his strategy to require escort fighters. The Eighth Air Force seized the air and never looked back, setting the conditions for the ensuing ground invasion six months later, in June 1944.

The final stop involved America's most recent conflict with Iraq. Here, Secretary of Defense Rumsfeld wanted to leverage advanced technologies and concepts to inculcate his transformation agenda in the Pentagon, transitioning the military from a garrison force to a lighter, rapidly deployable force. Engaging in the Iraq War offered a second proving ground, with a quick entry and exit strategy, for the lighter force articulated in

85

the "rapid dominance" concept. As recent history illustrated, while the smaller force had no issues with the third-world military power, it was unprepared for the large-scale insurgency that followed in a protracted eight and a half year struggle. Time will tell if the sacrifices in American blood and treasure advanced the causes espoused by the nation's leaders.

Analysis of each case study concluded that in all four examples, the specific steps a leader took to build advocacy for his erroneous decision was the result of individual and group cognitive errors, resulting in rigid thinking. These biases are not exclusive to the leaders discussed in these case studies. They persist today. In think tanks and planning cells across the globe, leaders and planning staffs continue to fall for these and other biases, resulting in rigid thinking, flawed decisions and increased risk in meeting national and military objectives. This is particularly hazardous in today's complex and dynamic security environment. Recommendations therefore focused on increasing adaptability in elements common to all case studies: the organization, the leader, and doctrine.

Organizationally, recommendations included institutionalizing hard-won adaptability skills learned in Iraq across the military, ensuring heterogeneity in planning and strategy cells to prevent groupthink, and implementing training on metacognition, heuristics, and cognitive biases in formal PME. Individual recommendations focused on leader development, with emphasis on not using history to validate a preconceived strategy stamped with doctrinal authority, embracing uncertainty to better confront the strategic environment, and increasing awareness of frames of reference and mental flexibility. Finally, doctrinal recommendations centered on maintaining the primacy of doctrine in decision making, augmenting current linear planning doctrine with nonlinear methods suggested by reflection-in-action and other adult learning theories, and the need for doctrine writers to acknowledge and counter cognitive biases as they write doctrine, hoping they do not get it *too wrong* so the military can adapt quickly in a future conflict.

From an expansive field of cognitive errors, "anchoring" and "confirmation bias" have perhaps the most applicability to the military leader, strategist, and tactician due to the relationship between military history, strategy, and doctrine. Given the tendency to employ heuristics in decision-making, subsequent research could focus on other cognitive biases. Efforts to expand the literature of how and why leaders think, their susceptibility to decision error, and the impact of this reality on military operations would continue to expand the awareness and potentially mitigate the negative impacts of this very human condition. Additional research could look at other group pathologies, again in an effort to expand the knowledge base of leaders and decision-makers in the military.

War is a complex problem with complex causes and an endless array of variables. No single factor, including individual or group biases, explains why a strategy succeeds or fails. The belief that "we fail because we tend to make a small mistake here, a small mistake there, and these mistakes add up" has universal applicability.[1] Ultimately, *how* leaders think through a problem is more important than *what* facts or knowledge they assimilate. "Expertise is necessary, [even] essential…but it is not sufficient. Far more important is how people approach and solve problems."[2] An awareness of cognitive biases, as well as the development of organizational adaptability and individual mental flexibility will help leaders guard against "great ideas," enabling them to remain objective as they develop plans and strategies for the next war.

---

[1] Dietrich Dörner, *The Logic of Failure: Why Things Go Wrong and What We Can Do to Make Them Right* (New York: Metropolitan Books, 1996), 6, 9.
[2] Shore, *Blunder*, 203.

BIBLIOGRAPHY

Books and Theses

Arnold, Henry H. *Global Mission.* Blue Ridge Summit, PA: TAB Books Inc, 1989.

Biddle, Tami Davis. *Rhetoric and Reality in Air Warfare: The Evolution of British and American Ideas About Strategic Bombing, 1914-1945*. Princeton, NJ: Princeton University Press, 2002.

Bloch, Marc. *Strange Defeat*. Translated by Gerard Hopkins. New York: Octagon Books, 1968.

Bond, Brian and Martin Alexander. "Liddell Hart and De Gaulle: The Doctrines of Limited Liability and Mobile Defense." In *Makers of Modern Strategy from Machiavelli to the Nuclear Age*, edited by Peter Paret, Gordon A. Craig, and Felix Gilbert, 598-623. Princeton, NJ: Princeton University Press, 1986.

Bowman, Martin W. *The Mighty Eighth at War: USAAF 8th Air Force Bombers Versus the Luftwaffe, 1943-1945*. Barnsley, Yorkshire: Pen & Sword Aviation, 2010.

Builder, Carl H. *The Icarus Syndrome: The Role of Air Power Theory in the Evolution and Fate of the U.S. Air Force*. New Brunswick, NJ: Transaction Publishers, 1994.

Cable, Larry E. *Conflict of Myths: The Development of American Counterinsurgency Doctrine and the Vietnam War*. New York: New York University Press, 1986.

Carroll, James J. "Physiological Problems of bomber Crews in the Eighth Air Force During WWII." Master's thesis, Air Command and Staff College, 1997. http:// www.dtic. mil/cgi-bin/GetTRDoc?AD=ADA398044 (accessed April 5, 2012).

Citino, Robert M. *From Blitzkrieg to Desert Storm: the Evolution of Operational Warfare*. Lawrence, KS: University Press of Kansas, 2004.

Clark, Wesley K. *Waging Modern War: Bosnia, Kosovo, and the Future of Combat,* rev. ed. New York: Public Affairs, 2002.

Clausewitz, Carl von. *On War*. Edited and translated by Michael Howard and Peter Paret. Princeton, NJ: Princeton University Press, 1976.

Clodfelter, Mark A. "Molding Airpower Convictions: Development and Legacy of William Mitchell's Strategic Thought." In *Paths of Heaven: The Evolution of Airpower Theory*, edited by Phillip S. Meilinger, 79-114. Maxwell Air Force Base, AL: Air University Press, 1997.

————. *The Limits of Airpower – The American Bombing of North Vietnam.* Lincoln, NB: University of Nebraska Press, 2006.

Cohen, Eliot S. and John Gooch. *Military Misfortunes – The Anatomy of Failure in War.* New York: The Free Press, 1990.

Coram, Robert. *Boyd: The Fighter Pilot Who Changed the Art of War.* Boston: Little, Brown, 2002.

Correll, John T. "Daylight Precision Bombing." *Air Force Magazine.* October 20, 2008. http://www.airforce-magazine.com/MagazineArchive/Documents/2008/October%202008/1008daylight.pdf (accessed April 7, 2012).

Corum, James S. "A Clash of Military Cultures: German and French Approaches to Technology Between the World Wars." USAF Academy Symposium, Colorado Springs, CO, September 1994. http://www.au.af.mil/au/awc/awcgate/saas/corum.pdf (accessed March 4, 2012).

Craven, Wesley Frank and James Lea Cate. *The Army Air Forces in World War II, Volume 1, Plans and Early Operations, January 1939 to August 1942.* Chicago: The University of Chicago Press, 1948.

de Gaulle, Charles. *War Memoirs, Volume I: The Call to Honour 1940-1942.* London: Weidenfeld and Nicolson, 1955.

Dörner, Dietrich. *The Logic of Failure: Why Things Go Wrong and What We Can Do to Make Them Right.* New York: Metropolitan Books, 1996.

Doughty, Robert A. "The Evolution of French Military Doctrine." Master's thesis, U.S. Army Command and General Staff College, 1976. http://www.scribd.com/doc/8033074/Evolution-of-French-Army-Doctrine-19191939 (accessed January 14, 2012).

————. *The Evolution of US Army Tactical Doctrine, 1946-76.* Fort Leavenworth, KS: Combat Studies Institute, U.S. Army Command and General Staff College, 1979. http://usacac.army.mil/cac2/cgsc/carl/resources/csi/Doughty/doughty.asp (accessed October 11, 2012).

————. *The Seeds of Disaster: The Development of French Army Doctrine, 1919-1939.* Hamden, CN: Archon Books, 1985.

————. *The Breaking Point: Sedan and the Fall of France, 1940.* Hamden, CT: Archon Books, 1990.

Douhet, Giulio. *The Command of the Air.* Washington, DC: Office of Air Force History, 1983.

Drew, Dennis and Don Snow. "Military Doctrine." In *Making Strategy, An Introduction to National Security Processes and Problems*, 163-174. Maxwell Air Force Base, AL: Air University Press, 1988.

Eslinger, Robert A. "The Neglect of Long-Range Escort Development During the Interwar Years." Master's thesis, Air Command and Staff College, 1997. http://www.dtic.mil/cgi-bin/GetTRDoc?AD= ADA393237 (accessed April 5, 2012).

Evans, Jonathan St. B.T. *Bias in Human Reasoning: Causes and Consequence.* Hillsdale, NJ: Lawrence Erlbaum Associates, 1989.

Faber, Peter R. "Interwar U.S. Army Aviation and The Air Corps Tactical School: Incubators of American Airpower," In *Paths of Heaven: The Evolution of Airpower Theory*, edited by Phillip S. Meilinger, 183-238. Maxwell Air Force Base, AL: Air University Press, 1997.

Fallows, James M. *Blind into Baghdad: America's War in Iraq*. New York: Vintage Books, 2006.

Frankland, Noble. *Bomber Offensive: Devastation of Europe*. New York: Ballantine Books, 1970.

Franks, Tommy. *American Soldier.* New York: Regan Books, 2004.

Freeman, Roger A., Alan Crouchman, and Vic Maslen. *Mighty Eighth War Diary.* London: Jane's, 1981.

Frey, Dieter, Stefan Shulz-Hardt, and Dagmar Stahlberg. "Information Seeking Among Individuals and Groups and Possible Consequences for Decision Making in Business and Politics." In *Understanding Group Behavior: Small Group Processes and Interpersonal Relations, Volume 2.* Mahwah, NJ: Lawrence Erlbaum Associates, Inc., 1996.

Gabow, Greg A. "Schweinfurt Raids and the Pause in Daylight Strategic Bombing." Master's thesis, U.S. Army Command and General Staff College, 2008. http://www.dtic.mil/cgi-bin/GetTRDoc?AD=ADA482986 (accessed March 18, 2011).

Gilbert, Martin. *The First World War: A Complete History.* New York: Henry Holt and Co., 1994.

Gilovich, Thomas. *How We Know What Isn't So: The Fallibility of Human Reason in Everyday Life.* New York: The Free Press, 1991.

Gladwell, Malcolm. *The Tipping Point: How Little Things Can Make a Big Difference.* Boston, MA: Little, Brown and Co., 2002.

———. *Blink: The Power of Thinking Without Thinking*. New York: Little, Brown and Co., 2005.

Gordon, Michael R. and Trainor, Bernard E. *Cobra II: The Inside Story of the Invasion and Occupation of Iraq*. New York: Pantheon Books, 2006.

Greenfield, Kent R. *American Strategy in World War II: A Reconsideration*. Baltimore: Johns Hopkins Press, 1963.

Greer, Thomas H. *The Development of Air Doctrine in the Army Air Arm 1917-1941*. Washington, DC: Office of Air Force History, United States Air Force, 1985.

Hafner, Ferdinand. "Cognitive Biases and Structural Failures in United States Foreign Policy: Explaining Decision-Making Dissonance in Phase IV Policy and Plans for Iraq." Master's thesis, Naval Postgraduate School, 2007. http://www.dtic.mil/dtic/tr/fulltext/u2/ a475957.pdf (accessed February 22, 2012).

Hammes, Thomas X. *The Sling and the Stone: On War in the 21st Century*. New York: Zenith Press, 2004.

Hansell, Haywood S. *The Strategic Air War against Germany*. Washington, DC: Office of Air Force History, 1986.

Herring, George C. *The Pentagon Papers*. New York: McGraw-Hill, 1993.

Herspring, Dale R. *The Pentagon and the Presidency: Civil-Military Relations from FDR to George W. Bush*. Lawrence, KS: University Press of Kansas, 2005.

Hess, Gary R. *Vietnam: Explaining America's Lost War*. Malden, MA: Blackwell Publishing, 2009.

Hilsman, Roger. *To Move a Nation*. Garden City, NY: Doubleday and Co., 1967.

Holley, Irving B. *Technology and Military Doctrine*. Maxwell Air Force Base, AL: Air University Press, 2004.

Howard, James R. "Preparing for War, Stumbling for Peace." Master's thesis, U.S. Army Command and Staff College, 2004. http://www.dtic.mil/cgi-bin/GetTRDoc?AD=ADA430508 (accessed January 21, 2012).

Hunsaker, Kirk W. "The Invincible Bomber: Perspectives on the Recognition and Prevention of Airpower Crisis." Master's thesis, Air University, 2005. http://www.dtic.mil/cgi-bin/GetTRDoc?AD=ADA477072 (accessed February 11, 2012).

Janis, Irving L. *Groupthink: Psychological Studies of Policy Decisions and Fiascos*, 2nd rev. ed. Boston: Houghton Mifflin, 1983.

Johnson, Dominic D. P. *Overconfidence and War: The Havoc and Glory of Positive Illusions*. Cambridge, MA: Harvard University Press, 2004. http://site.ebrary.com/lib/nationaldefense/Doc?id=10314232 (accessed March 4, 2012).

Keegan, John. *The Iraq War*. New York: Alfred A. Knopf, Random House, Inc., 2004.

Kiesling, Eugenia C. *Arming Against Hitler: France and the Limits of Military Planning*. Lawrence, KS: University of Kansas Press, 1996.

Kimball, Warren F., ed. *Churchill and Roosevelt: The Complete Correspondence*, Volume 1. Princeton, NJ: Princeton University Press, 1984.

Kolb, David A. *Experiential Learning: Experience as the Source of Learning and Development*. Englewood Cliffs, NJ: Prentice-Hall, 1984.

Krepinevich, Andrew. *The Army and Vietnam*. Baltimore, MD: Johns Hopkins University Press, 1986.

Lawrence, T.E. *Seven Pillars of Wisdom: A Triumph*. 1935. Reprint, New York: First Anchor Books, 1991.

Linn, Brian McAllister. *The Echo of Battle: The Army's Way of War*. Cambridge, MA: Harvard University Press, 2007.

Long, Austin G. Doctrine of Eternal Recurrence The U.S. Military and Counterinsurgency Doctrine, 1960-1970 and 2003-2006. Santa Monica, CA: Rand National Defense Research Institute, 2008. http://www.rand.org/pubs/ occasional_papers/2008/ RAND_OP200.pdf (accessed November 10, 2011).

MacIsaac, David. *Strategic Bombing in World War Two: The Story of the United States Strategic Bombing Survey*. New York: Garland Publishing Co., 1976.

Mann, James. *Rise of the Vulcans: The History of Bush's War Cabinet*. New York: Viking Penguin, 2004.

Mclintock, Michael. *Instruments of Statecraft: U.S. Guerrilla Warfare, Counterinsurgency, and Counterterrorism*, 1940-1990. New York: Pantheon Books, 1992.

McManus, John C. *Grunts: Inside the American Infantry Combat Experience, World War II Through Iraq*. New York: New American Library, 2010.

McMaster, H.R. "Crack in the Foundation." Master's thesis, U.S. Army War College, 2003. http://www.csl.army.mil/usacsl/Publications/S03-03.pdf (accessed February 12, 2012).

Meilinger, Phillip S. "Giulio Douhet and the Origins of Airpower Theory." In *Paths of Heaven: The Evolution of Air Power Theory*, edited by Phillip S. Meilinger, 1-40. Maxwell Air Force Base, AL: Air University Press, 1987.

———. "Trenchard, Slessor, and the RAF doctrine before WWII." In *Paths of Heaven: The Evolution of Air Power Theory*, edited by Phillip S. Meilinger, 41-78. Maxwell Air Force Base, AL: Air University Press, 1987.

Middlebrook, Martin. *The Schweinfurt-Regensburg Mission*. New York: Charles Scribner's Sons, 1983.

Miller, Donald L. *Masters of the Air: America's Bomber Boys Who Fought the Air War Against Nazi Germany*. New York: Simon & Schuster, 2006.

Millett, Allan R. and Williamson Murray. *Military Innovation in the Interwar Period*. New York: Cambridge University Press, 1996.

———. *Military Effectiveness: Volume 2, The Interwar Years*. New York: Cambridge University Press, 2010.

Murray, Williamson and Robert H. Scales. *The Iraq War: A Military History*. Cambridge, MA: Harvard University Press, 2003.

Owens, William A., and Edward Offley. *Lifting the Fog of War*. New York: Farrar, Straus and Giroux, 2000.

Parton, James. *"Air Force Spoken Here": General Ira Eaker and the Command of the Air*. Bethesda, MD: Alder & Alder, Publishers, Inc., 1986.

Perret, Geoffrey. *Winged Victory: the Army Air Force in World War II*. New York: Random House Inc, 1993.

Ricks, Thomas. *Fiasco: The American Military Adventure in Iraq*. New York: The Penguin Press, 2006.

Romjue, John L. *From Active Defense to AirLand Battle: The Development of Army Doctrine 1973-1982*. Fort Monroe, VA: United States Army Training and Doctrine Command, 1984.

Rosen, Barry A. *The Sources of Military Doctrine*. Ithaca, NY: Cornell University Press, 1984.

Rumsfeld, Donald. *Known and Unknown: A Memoir*. New York: Sentinel, 2011.

Schafer, Mark and Scott Crichlow. *Groupthink Versus High-Quality Decision Making in International Relations*. New York: Columbia University Press, 2010.

Scheeringa, Daniel. "Was the Decision to Invade Iraq and the Failure of Occupation Planning a Case of Groupthink?" Master's thesis, Virginia Polytechnic Institute, 2010. http://scholar.lib.vt.edu/ theses/ available/etd-07292010-145020/ unrestricted/ Scheeringa_DJ_T-2010.pdf (accessed March 4, 2012)

Serena, Chad C. *A Revolution in Military Adaptation: The U.S. Army in the Iraq War.* Washington, DC: Georgetown University Press, 2011.

Seyer, Sean H. "The Plan Put into Practice: USAAF Bombing Doctrine and the Ploesti Campaign." Master's thesis, University of Missouri – St. Louis, 2009. http://auburn.academia.edu/SeanSeyer/Papers/451576/The_plan_put_into_practice_USAAF_bombing_doctrine_and_the_Ploesti_campaign (accessed April 4, 2011).

Shimko, Keith L. *The Iraqi Wars and America's Military Revolution.* Cambridge, MA: Cambridge University Press, 2010.

Shore, Zachary. *Blunder: Why Smart People Make Bad Decisions.* New York: Bloomsbury, 2008.

Simon, Herbert A. *Administrative Behavior*, 4th ed. New York: Simon and Schuster, 1997.

Steihm, Judith. *The U.S. Army War College: Military Education and Democracy.* Philadelphia, PA: Temple University Press, 2002.

Sweetman, John. *Schweinfurt: Disaster in the Skies.* New York: Ballantine Books, 1971.

Taylor, John M. *An American Soldier: The Wars of General Maxwell Taylor.* Novato, CA: Presidio Press, Inc., 1989.

Terdoslavich, William. "From Shock and Awe to Aw Shucks." In *Beyond Shock and Awe: Warfare in the 21st Century, 11-63.* New York: Berkley Caliber, 2006.

Thompson, W. Scott, and Donaldson D. Frizzell. *The Lessons of Vietnam.* New York: Crane, Russak and Co., 1977.

Tse-Tung, Mao. On Guerrilla Warfare. Translated by Samuel B. Griffith III. Urbana, IL: University of Illinois Press, 2000.

Ullman, Harlan K. and James P. Wade. *Shock and Awe: Achieving Rapid Dominance.* Washington, DC: NDU Press Book, 1996. http://www.dtic.mil/cgi-bin/GetTRDoc?AD=ADA457606&Location=U2&doc=GetTRDoc.pdf (accessed May 30, 2012).

Warden, John A. III. *The Air Campaign: Planning for Combat.* Washington, DC: Pergamon-Brassey's, 1989.

Watts, Barry D. *The Foundations of U.S. Air Doctrine: The Problem of Friction in War.* Maxwell Air Force Base, AL: Air University Press, 1984.

Webster, Charles and Noble Frankland. *The Strategic Air Offensive Against Germany 1939-1945.* London: Her Majesty's Stationary Office, 1961.

Westmoreland, William C. *A Soldier Reports.* Garden City, NY: Doubleday and Company, Inc, 1976.

Winton, Harry R. and Davis, R. Mets. *The Challenge of Change - Military Institutions and New Realities, 1918-1941.* Lincoln, NB: University of Nebraska Press, 2000.

Woodward, Bob. *Plan of Attack.* New York: Simon and Schuster, 2004.

——— . *State of Denial: Bush at War, Part III.* New York: Simon and Schuster, 2006.

Zaloga, Steve. *Panzer IV vs Char B1 Bis: France 1940.* Oxford: Osprey Pub, 2011.

Zucchino, David. *Thunder Run: The Armored Strike to Capture Baghdad.* New York: Grove Press, 2004.

Academic Journals, Papers, and Presentations

Ahlstrom, David and Linda C. Wang. "Groupthink and France's Defeat in the 1940 Campaign." *Journal of Management History* 15, no. 2 (2009): 159-177.

Chisholm, Donald. "The Risk of Optimism in the Conduct of War." *Parameters: U.S. Army War College Quarterly 33,* no. 4 (2004): 114-131. http://www.carlisle.army .mil/usawc/parameters/Articles/03winter/chisholm.pdf (accessed March 11, 2012).

Echevarria, Antulio J. II. "The Trouble with History." *Parameters: U.S. Army War College Quarterly,* 35, no. 2 (2005): 78-90. http://www.carlisle.army.mil/usawc/ parameters/Articles/05summer/echevarr.pdf (accessed February 13, 2012).

Herek, Gregory M., Irving L. Janis, and Paul Huth. "Decision making during international crisis: Is quality of process related to outcome?" *Journal of Conflict Resolution* 31, no.2 (June 1987): 203-26. http://www.jstor.org/stable/174011 (accessed February 25, 2012).

Hilgevoord, Jan. "The Uncertainty Principle for Energy and Time." *American Journal of Physics* 64, no. 12 (December 1996). http://www.stat.physik.unipotsdam.de/ ~pikovsky/teaching/stud_seminar/ ajp_uncert_energy_time1.pdf (accessed February 27, 2012).

Howard, Michael. "Military Science in the Age of Peace." *RUSI Journal* 119, (March 1974): 3-9.

———. "The Use and Abuse of Military History." *The Army Doctrine and Training Bulletin* 6, no. 2 (Summer 2003): 18-22. http://www.army.forces.gc.ca/caj/ documents/ vol_06/iss_2/ CAJ_vol6.2_06_e.pdf (accessed February 24, 2012).

Jaques, Eliot. "The Development of Intellectual Capability: A Discussion of Stratified Systems Theory." *The Journal of Applied Behavioral Science* 22 (October 1986): 361-383.

Kahneman, Daniel and Amos Tversky. "Judgment under Uncertainty: Heuristics and Biases." *Science, New Series* 185, no. 4157 (September 27, 1974): 1124-1131. http://www.jstor.org/stable/1738360 (accessed February 21, 2012).

Lindblom, Charles E. "The Science of "Muddling Through." *Public Administration Review* 19 (Spring 1959): 79-88. http://www.archonfung.net/docs/temp/ LindblomMuddlingThrough1959.pdf (accessed April 16, 2012).

Mansoor, Peter R. "The Second Battle of Sedan, May 1940." *Military Review* 68 (June 1988): 64-75. http://cgsc.cdmhost.com/cdm/singleitem/collection/p124201coll1/ id/514/ rec/2704 (accessed January 7, 2012).

Paparone, Christopher R. "The Reflective Military Practitioner: How Military Professionals Think in Action." *Military Review* 88 no. 2 (March-April 2008): 66-76. http://www.au.af.mil/au/awc/awcgate/milreview/paparone_mar08.pdf (accessed February 26, 2012).

Schafer, Mark and Scott Crichlow. "Antecedents of Groupthink: A Quantitative Study." *The Journal of Conflict Resolution* 40 no. 3, (September 1996): 415-35. http://www.jstor.org/stable/view/174313 (accessed February 25, 2012).

Taber, Charles S. and Milton Lodge. "Motivated Skepticism in the Evaluation of Political Beliefs." *American Journal of Political Science* 50, no. 3 (July 2006): 755-769. http://www.unc.edu/~fbaum/teaching/POLI891_Sp11/articles/AJPS-2006-Taber.pdf (accessed February 21, 2012).

Turner, Marlene and Anthony Pratkanis. "Twenty-five Years of Groupthink Theory and Research: Lessons from the Evaluation of a Theory." *Organizational Behavior and Human Decision Processes* 73 nos.2/3 (February-March 1998): 107-108. http://carmine.se.edu/cvonbergen/Twenty-Five%20Years%20of%20Groupthink% 20Theory%20and%20Research_Lessons%20from%20the%20Evaluation%20of% 20a%20Theory.pdf (accessed March 7, 2012).

Ullman, Harlan. "Shock and Awe Revisited." RUSI Journal 148, no. 3 (2003): 10-14. http://ezproxy6.ndu.edu/login?url=http://search.proquest.com/docview/21212359 6?accountid=12686. (accessed October 14, 2011).

Williams, Blair S. "Heuristics and Biases in Military Decision Making." *Military Review* 90 no. 5 (September-October 2010): 40-52. http://www.au.af.mil/au/ awc/ awcgate/milreview/williams_ bias_mil_d-m.pdf (accessed February 26, 2012).

Magazine Articles (Print and Online)

Barrett, David M. "Doing 'Tuesday Lunch' at Lyndon Johnson's White House: New Archival Evidence on Vietnam Decisionmaking." *Political Science and Politics* 24, No. 4 (December 1991): 677. http://www.jstor.org/stable/419403 (accessed March 4, 2012).

Hersh, Seymour M. "Selective Intelligence: Donald Rumsfeld has his own special sources. Are they reliable?" *The New Yorker*, 12 May 2003. http://www.new yorker.com/ archive/2003/05/12/030512fa_fact (accessed December 11, 2011).

Online Resources

Choo, Chun Wei. "Groupthink Theoretical Framework." University of Toronto. http://choo.fis.utoronto.ca/FIS/courses/lis2149/Groupthink.html (accessed April 9, 2012).

Dwyer, Larry. "Boeing B-17 Flying Fortress." The Aviation History Online Museum. http://www.aviation-history.com/ boeing/b17.html (accessed February 26, 2012).

Henman, Linda. "How to Avoid the Hidden Traps of Decision Making." The Henman Performance Group. http://www.henmanperformancegroup.com (accessed February 21, 2012).

iCasualties.org. "Iraq Coalition Casualty Count." iCasualties.org. http://www.defense.gov/news/casualty.pdf (accessed December 21, 2011).

Kopelman, Richard E. and Anne L. Davis. "A Demonstration of the Anchoring Effect." The Decision Sciences Journal of Innovative Education. http://kelley.iupui.edu/ dsjie/Tips/kopelman.htm (accessed February 21, 2012).

Lone Sentry. "Firing Tables – Technical Manual E9-369A: German 88-mm Antiaircraft Gun Materiel." Lone Sentry. http://www.lonesentry.com/manuals/88mm-antiaircraft-gun/german-88-mm-firing-tables.html (accessed February 26, 2012).

97

Schwartz, Mel. "Order Out of Chaos—Learning to Embrace Uncertainty." Psychology Today. http://www.psychologytoday.com/blog/shift-mind/200811/order-out-chaos-learning-embrace-uncertainty-part-1 (accessed February 26, 2012).

Trautman, Tim M. "FAQs about Army Air Force Terms in WWII." 398th Bomb Group Memorial Association. http://www.398th.org/Research/398th_FAQ.html#anchor_mission (accessed January 14, 2012).

Government Reports

U.S. Department of the Air Force. *Air Force Basic Doctrine, Organization, and Command, Air Force Doctrine Document 1.* Maxwell Air Force Base, AL: Lemay Center for Doctrine Development and Education, October 14, 2011.

U.S. Department of the Army. *Counterguerrilla Operations, FM 31-16.* Washington, DC: Department of the Army, February, 1963.

———. *Field Service Regulations, Operations, FM 100-5.* Washington, DC: Department of the Army, 1962.

U.S. Department of State. *Foreign Relations of the United States, 1961-1963, Volume I, Vietnam 1961.* Washington, DC: Government Printing Office, 1988.

U.S. Joint Chiefs of Staff. *Department of Defense Dictionary of Military and Associated Terms, Joint Publication 1-02.* Washington, DC: Joint Chiefs of Staff, October 15, 2011.

U.S. Joint Forces Command. *The Joint Operating Environment (JOE) 2010.* Suffolk, VA: U.S. Joint Forces Command, February 17, 2010).

VITA

Lieutenant Colonel Yancy is a 1992 graduate of the United States Air Force Academy with a Bachelor of Science in Management. Colonel Yancy is a command pilot with over 2,700 hours in the F-15C, F-117A, and F-22A. He holds a Master of Aeronautical Science from Embry Riddle University and a Master of Military Operational Art and Science from Air Command and Staff College. Prior to attending the Joint Advanced Warfighting School, Colonel Yancy served as the Deputy Commander, 49th Operations Group at Holloman Air Force Base, New Mexico.

www.ingramcontent.com/pod-product-compliance
Lightning Source LLC
Chambersburg PA
CBHW081839280526
45789CB00007B/2507